Play Bridge in Four Hours

Play Bridge in Four Hours

Peter Steinberg

GROSSET & DUNLAP
A FILMWAYS COMPANY
Publishers • New York

For Morris and Minnie Yellen,
Martin and Susan Snow and, of
course, for Leon.

Published simultaneously in Canada

Library of Congress catalog card number: 77-94853

ISBN 0-448-14673-8

First printing 1978

Printed in the United States of America

CONTENTS

ACKNOWLEDGMENTS

Thank you:

Jimmy Hamilton for teaching ME how to play bridge, way back when.
Temple Shaaray Tefila and Bertha Grebin for giving me my first
big teaching opportunity.
Howard Phalzer and Fran Zilberg (of J.A.S.A.) for my second major
teaching position and many good recommendations.
Lee Vines for making me head bridge instructor at the Old Colony
Bridge Club.
Kathie Wei for immeasurable help in introducing my new teaching
method.
Jim Becker and Mirette Mignocchi for bringing me to Manhattan's
biggest bridge club, The Beverly East Bridge Club.
Mel Skolnik for sound business advice, and good publicity regard-
ing my teaching method, bridge columns and articles, and also
this book.
The Brooklyn Heights Press, The Orange County Chronicle and The
Smithtown Messenger for printing my bridge columns.
And twenty-five hundred students, who through the years have had
the patience to sit through my classes.

For help in producing this book:

James Jacobson for marketing.
Oscar Collier and Lisa Collier for being "top drawer" literary
agents and Leslie Garisto for assisting them.
Diana Price, editor at Grosset, for knowledgeable assistance and
accessibility.
John Clement, copy editor, for an extremely competent job of
honing my material.
Judith Brown, editorial assistant, for typing services.

A special acknowledgment:

Nancy Lawrence, Kaz Nagamastu, Elaine Paul and Pat Rogers for
being old friends and my most treasured private class.

Bridge partners and friends:

Doug Herron, Bob True, Eric Berger, Bob Haven, Ron Felton, Bob
Ritta, Bob Umlas, Kal Weiss, Bob Glantz, Bea Lane, Elizabeth
Brenhouse, Milton Cohn, Ruth Bishop, Richard Jupa, Judy Simmons,
Greg Woods, Susan Kantar, Bob Poertz (the authority), Flo Wilnau,
Jared Lilienstein, and in memory of Sam Fisher and Al Harrison.

FOREWORD

For over fifty years I have believed firmly that an absolute beginner can only learn bridge by means of long and arduous study. The reason is that they have been taught by rote and by memorizing rule after rule.

This book offers a new teaching concept. It teaches beginners to do things, not to memorize rules.

Not that you don't have to use some memory here but you will actually be remembering something you have done, not something you expect to do some time in the future.

The good bridge teacher--and there are lots of good bridge teachers--spends hours and hours just going over the basic rules. What is a trick? Which card wins a trick? Who leads the first trick? Who leads to later tricks? And so on.

PLAY BRIDGE IN FOUR HOURS should make it possible for a teacher to get into the nitty gritty of actual play in one tenth the time it normally takes. This won't hurt the teacher at all. It will just let him teach more bridge so that his pupils will get a lot more value per lesson.

As for you, the person who wants to learn bridge by himself or a group who wants to learn without going to a teacher, this book will open the whole vista of bridge to you in just a few hours.

Oswald Jacoby

INTRODUCTION

I first met Peter Steinberg eight years ago in a New York City bridge club. He told me that the night before he had tried to teach a friend how to play bridge and it had been a disaster. It is a story, with variations, I have heard repeated many times since.

The group Steinberg was with needed a fourth. Peter asked his friend to sit in. He protested he had never played before, but Peter assured him it would be all right. He gave his friend a crash course and they sat down to play. What happened is still recalled with glee by the opponents and with embarrassment by Peter and his friend.

On the first hand it was the friend's turn to bid. "What should I do?" he asked.

"Bid your best suit," Peter said.
"What do you mean?"
"Just tell me what your best suit is."
He thought for several minutes. "I guess," he finally said, "that my best suit is the blue one I wore last Sunday."

The opposing partnership could not stop laughing, the humiliated friend stormed out, and the bridge game was over.

Peter Steinberg will never relive this scene. He has since become one of the most respected teachers in the country and gives lessons at the prestigious Beverly Bridge Club in Manhattan. Some of the best players in the world come to Peter for advice, but it is with the teaching of beginners that he has no peer. PLAY BRIDGE IN FOUR HOURS is like having Peter at your side teaching the game, yet it is much less expensive and the book will always be there as an important reference.

It should be clear that I could not be more impressed by this revolutionary teaching book. It is easy to read, beautifully diagrammed. Most importantly, it completely fulfills its purpose: it turns the absolute beginner into a reasonable player in four hours.

I am going to give several copies of this book to friends. I expect they will be gifts that will be valued for a long time because they will introduce the readers to a marvelous and stimulating pastime.

When I first stood over Peter's shoulder listening to him teach a bridge class, I wished there could be twenty Peter Steinbergs. That way twenty times as many people could benefit from his unique methods of instruction.

His book solves the problem.

Alan Sontag

How to use this book:

The first four hours (pages 1 - 104) will teach you how to play bridge. The last half of this book will teach you how to play well.

Don't spend too much time on any one part and don't try to memorize anything.

Just read the explanations and play through all game situations which are provided on worksheets.

After completing each section, break before moving on. I recommend that you do only one section per evening, but of course you can proceed faster if you wish.

You should finish each chapter almost as fast as it would take for a normal reading.

COMING UP:

How to Play Bridge

Recommended time: 20 to 30 minutes

Before we examine how bridge is played, I would like to teach you a children's game called war.

A deck of cards is divided between two people who stack their cards face down in front of them. Then each player turns the top one over, hoping to beat his opponent. The winner adds both cards to the bottom of his pile and the process is repeated until someone is out.

There is a little more to it, of course, but basically whoever has the highest card wins, and bridge is very much the same.

In its simplest form, bridge is no more than war played by four people.

The players sit around a card table, and for convenience, we'll call them South, West, North and East. One player, let's say South, will shuffle and deal out a deck of cards until all 52 are distributed equally around the table. All cards are dealt one at a time, beginning with the person to the dealer's left (this time West) and ending with the dealer.

Remember, the cards are dealt in a clockwise direction. In fact, everything in bridge is always done clockwise!

After the deal, the first thing you should do is count your cards (without looking at them) to make sure you have exactly 13. If anyone has more or less, the cards must be redistributed.

The cards are ranked as follows, from the highest to the lowest:

ace   (A)
king   (K)
queen (Q)
jack   (J)
ten   (10)
nine   (9)
eight (8)
seven (7)
six   (6)
five   (5)
four   (4)
three (3)
two   (2)

North

West   (table)   East

South

Next, pick up your hand* (each player's 13 cards are called a hand) and sort it into suits. Most people keep their hand separated by colors. They put the spades first, followed by hearts, clubs and diamonds. This is a good way to arrange it, but do whatever is best for you.

After counting and sorting, you are ready to begin playing. For now, we will play war, but after each deal a slight variation will be added, until you are playing bridge.

Try the first hand. We will call you South and you can lead the initial card.

Take any card from your hand and place it face up in the center of the table. West plays next and tries to beat your card; then North and East. The four cards that are now in the center of the table are called a trick and whoever played the highest card, wins the trick.

Just like war, except for one thing. Each player must play the same suit as the one which was originally led. If anyone is unable to follow, they must play a card of another suit, but have no chance to win the trick.

Only the highest card in the suit which was led can win the trick, and you must follow suit if you are able to do so.

Whoever wins a trick leads the first card to the next trick and the idea is to win as many tricks as possible.

*hand is also a collective term used to describe one deal of bridge

There are four suits:

    spades   (♠)
    hearts   (♡)
    diamonds (◊)
    clubs   (♣)

Each suit has 13 cards.

If you want to name any specific card, say king of hearts, jack of spades, two of clubs, etc.

Specific cards are written like this:

    ♡K (king of hearts)
    ♠J (jack of spades)
    ♣2 (two of clubs)
    ◊A (ace of diamonds)

If you were dealt the ace, king, queen of spades, the ten, nine, three, two of hearts, the five, four, three, two of diamonds and the five and two of clubs, your hand would be written like this:

    ♠ A K Q
    ♡ 10 9 3 2
    ◊ 5 4 3 2
    ♣ 5 2

After winning a trick, bunch the cards into one group, keeping it face down in front of you. When you win another, overlap that group on top of the first (and so on) to keep track of how many you've won.

The hand is over when all 52 cards have been played and who-ever has the most tricks is the winner.

Deal out another hand, but this time, imagine that your neighbor is sitting directly across from you. He will be your partner, and bridge is a partnership game. If he wins a trick, it's your trick, too.

Assume your partner leads the king of hearts (♡K). The next player follows with a small heart and now it's your turn to play.

If you have the ace of hearts (♡A) you'd better keep it, unless it's your only heart. Your partner's king is high enough to win the trick.

Only one player from each side keeps the partnership tricks in front of him.

When the hand is over, the partnership which has won the most tricks is the winner.

This is a bridge hand:

♠ A Q J 10
♡ K 9 6 3 2
♢ 7 6
♣ Q 2

This is also a bridge hand:

North

♠ A Q J 10
♡ K 9 6 3 2
♢ 7 6
♣ Q 2

West

♠ K 5 3 2
♡ 10 8 7
♢ K Q J 10
♣ K 4

East

♠ 8 7 6
♡ A Q
♢ 9 5 4 3 2
♣ A J 10

South

♠ 9 4
♡ J 5 4
♢ A 8
♣ 9 8 7 6 5 3

This hand encompasses all four individual hands.

Questions:

1. How many people are needed to play bridge?

2. What are the highest and lowest cards in the deck?

3. The cards are dealt in which direction?

4. After the cards have been dealt, what is the first thing you should do?

5. How many cards should be dealt to each person?

6. What should you do after picking up your hand?

7. What are the four suits?

8. How many cards make up a trick?

   For the next few questions, use the diagram in the enclosed column.

9. If South leads a card, who should play next?

10. If East wins a trick, who leads the first card to the next trick?

11. If you are South, who is your partner?

12. If East leads a spade, does South have to follow suit?

13. What if South has no spades?

14. If South has no spades, can he win the trick?

```
                North


West                        East


                South
```

Answers:

1. four.

2. The ace is the highest and the 2, the lowest.

3. clockwise.

4. count them.

5. 13.

6. sort it into suits.

7. spades, hearts, diamonds and clubs.

8. 4.

9. West.

10. East.

11. North.

12. yes; so do West and North.

13. If South has no spades, he must play a card from another suit.

14. He has no chance to win the trick.

Now you are ready to play bridge, and you can start by dealing out another hand.

Only one person will actually play the hand, and that person is called the declarer. You are still South and for this hand you are also the declarer.

The person to the declarer's left (in this case West) always leads the first card and is called the opening leader.

Otherwise, the play proceeds exactly as before; except for one thing.

After the opening lead has been placed in the center of the table, the declarer's partner (North) lays his hand face up in front of him so that all three of the other players can see it. The exposed hand is called the dummy, and the person who originally held it will not touch a card until the next deal.

The declarer will play both hands and the dummy should be arranged in suits in such a way that the declarer can read the cards without any trouble. This is done by laying each suit vertically, pointing toward the declarer. The highest card of each suit should be at the top, and no sequence of cards should be upside down to the declarer. The dummy's suits should be separated by color.

Once the opening lead has been made, dummy comes into view and the declarer takes over. He chooses which card the dummy plays by placing it in the

Remember, the dummy is always the hand opposite the declarer.

                    North

West   East

                    South

If South is the declarer, then North is the dummy and West will make the opening lead.

North and South are called the declaring side; West and East are called the defending side or the defenders.

If you hold this hand:

    ♠ K J 8 7
    ♡ 10 9 8 7
    ◊ K J 8
    ♣ 3 2

and later become the dummy, lay it down like this:

    ♠   ♡   ♣   ◊
    K   10   3   K
    J   9   2   J
    8   8   8
    7   7

center of the table and each person plays in turn until the trick is completed.

Whenever dummy wins a trick, lead the first card to the next trick from the dummy.

Remember, you play both hands until the game is over and it is still highest card wins.

And bridge is played just like that, except for one last thing.

Deal out ·another hand and count, sort, and let West make the opening lead. Now lay down the dummy. After looking it over, pick the suit which has the greatest number of cards between your hand and dummy's. Don't think about high cards, pick the longest suit between the two hands.

We will call this suit "trump."

Assume you picked hearts, so hearts are trump. You will play as before with one exception. This time if any player is unable to follow suit when his turn comes, he can win the trick by playing a heart.

Trump is just another name for wild card. If two players are unable to follow suit on the same trick and both play trump, the highest trump wins.

But it is not mandatory to play trump if you cannot follow suit to the trick in progress. You can play another suit and save your trump for later. For example, it would be foolish to trump a trick if you expect your partner to win it with a high card.

Here are some things to know about trump:

Play this hand:

Spades are trump!

North
♠ 4
♡ ---
♢ J
♣ 8

West
♠ 8
♡ J
♢ ---
♣ J

East
♠ ---
♡ 7
♢ 6
♣ 9

South
♠ ---
♡ 10
♢ 10
♣ A

This is not a complete hand, as most of the cards have already been played.

Whenever you see ---, it means there are no cards left in that suit.

South leads the ♡10 and West covers with the ♡J. North can win the trick by trumping with the ♠4.

If South leads a diamond, West can win by trumping because he has no diamonds.

South and East cannot trump anything because they have no trump.

Any of the four suits can be delegated as trump, and it is always wise for the declaring side to have more than their opponents.

A trump may be led at any time, including the first card played to any given trick. In fact, the declarer usually plays trump quickly to prevent his winners from being "trumped."

Remember, the lowly two of trump can capture an ace of another suit. Do you see why you want more trump than your opponents?

The trump suit is always laid down to dummy's far right, or as the declarer sees dummy, to his far left.

So put your trump suit in the right place, because that is the end. That is all there is to the mechanics of bridge play.

Of course, you won't always be the declarer. Sometimes your partner or one of the opponents will. And not every hand is played with a trump suit. Many times the hand will be played in notrump, or high card always wins.

Who declares the hand and whether or not there is a trump suit is determined before the play begins. Both partnerships will compete by bidding for the opportunity to play the hand.

The second chapter explains what bidding is, and how you can use it to find your trump suit.

Assume this is your hand,

    ♠ K J 9 7
    ♡ A 8 7 3 2
    ♢ Q J 10
    ♣ 8

and this is partner's.

    ♠ A Q 10
    ♡ 9 6 5 4
    ♢ K 5
    ♣ J 9 6 5

You want hearts to be trump because you have more of them than any other suit.

If your partner became the dummy, he would put his hand down like this:

♡	♠	♢	♣
9	A	K	J
6	Q	5	9
5	10		6
4			5

Notice that the hearts (trump) are to the far left as you look at the dummy.

Questions:

1. Who is the person who actually plays the hand?

2. What is his partner called?

3. When should the dummy lay his hand down?

4. Who makes the opening lead?

5. How should the dummy be arranged?

6. Who plays the dummy?

7. When dummy wins a trick, which hand leads the first card to the next trick?

8. If West is the declarer, who is the dummy? And who...

9. makes the opening lead?

10. What is another name for trump?

11. Treating your hand and dummy's as one unit, do you want your strongest or your longest suit to be trump?

12. When dummy comes down, where do trump go?

13. Can any suit be trump?

North

West   East

South

Answers:

1. the declarer.

2. the dummy.

3. after the opening lead.

4. the person to the declarer's left.

5. The suits should be arranged vertically, so that the declarer can easily read the cards.

6. the declarer.

7. the dummy.

8. East.

9. North.

10. wild card.

11. the longest.

12. at dummy's far right.

13. yes.

Now play these hands!

1.   South is the declarer and hearts are trump. As you see, most of the cards have already been played.

    South leads the ♠4.

    Who plays next?

    What card should West play?

    Suppose that West plays the ♠2 and South plays dummy's ♠A. Can East win this trick?

1.

          North

          ♠ A 3
          ♡ J
          ♢ ---
          ♣ ---

West   **East**

♠ K 2   ♠ ---
♡ 4   ♡ 8
♢ ---   ♢ ---
♣ ---   ♣ J 10

          South

          ♠ 8 6 4
          ♡ ---
          ♢ ---
          ♣ ---

2.   West is the declarer and there is no trump suit. West leads the ♠J.

    Who plays next?

    North follows with the ♠Q, East (dummy) plays the ♠K and South wins the trick with the ♠A.

    Who leads the first card to the next trick?

    What card should he lead?

    If South plays correctly, how many tricks will North/South win?

2.

          North

          ♠ Q
          ♡ ---
          ♢ 6
          ♣ J

West   **East**

♠ J 10   ♠ K 3
♡ ---   ♡ ---
♢ ---   ♢ A
♣ 2   ♣ ---

          South

          ♠ A
          ♡ 2
          ♢ Q
          ♣ ---

Analysis:

1.

North
♠ A 3
♡ J
♢ ---
♣ ---

West
♠ K 2
♡ 4
♢ ---
♣ ---

East
♠ ---
♡ 8
♢ ---
♣ J 10

South
♠ 8 6 4
♡ ---
♢ ---
♣ ---

<u>Hearts</u> <u>are</u> <u>trump</u>!

After South leads the ♠4, West will play next.

West should play the ♠2. Remember, North is the dummy and everyone at the table can see its cards. If West plays the ♠K, he knows he will lose it to dummy's ace.

Even though South plays dummy's ♠A, East can win this trick by trumping it with the ♡8.

2.

North
♠ Q
♡ ---
♢ 6
♣ J

West
♠ J 10
♡ ---
♢ ---
♣ 2

East
♠ K 3
♡ ---
♢ A
♣ ---

South
♠ A
♡ 2
♢ Q
♣ ---

<u>There</u> <u>is</u> <u>no</u> <u>trump</u> <u>suit</u>.

After West leads the ♠J, North will play next.

South wins the first trick with the ♠A, and therefore leads the first card to the next trick.

South should lead the ♡2 because nobody else has any hearts. Remember, this is notrump and if no one can follow suit, the tiny two will win the trick. Note that if South leads instead the ◊Q, East/West will win the rest.of the tricks.

North/South should win 2 out of 3 tricks.

3. South is the declarer and diamonds are trump.

Which hand is the dummy?

South leads the ♠8, West covers with the ♠A and North trumps it with the ◊9.

Can East win this trick?

How?

3.

North
♠ ---
♡ ---
◊ 9
♣ A 6

West
♠ A 4 3
♡ ---
◊ ---
♣ ---

East
♠ ---
♡ ---
◊ 10
♣ 8 7

South
♠ 8
♡ ---
◊ J 7
♣ ---

4. South is the declarer and clubs are trump.

South leads the ♡10 and West, having no clubs to trump it with, discards the ♠2. North (dummy) must play the ♠J.

Obviously, this trick belongs to East. Which card should he win it with?

What card should East lead to the next trick?

If East plays correctly, how many tricks will East/West win?

4.

North
♠ 5
♡ J
◊ ---
♣ J

West
♠ K 3 2
♡ ---
◊ ---
♣ ---

East
♠ ---
♡ A Q
◊ ---
♣ K

South
♠ ---
♡ K 10
◊ ---
♣ Q

Analysis:

3.

North
♠ ---
♡ ---
◇ 9
♣ A 6

West
♠ A 4 3
♡ ---
◇ ---
♣ ---

East
♠ ---
♡ ---
◇ 10
♣ 8 7

South
♠ 8
♡ ---
◇ J 7
♣ ---

Diamonds are trump!

If South is the declarer, North must be the dummy.

South leads the ♠8, West covers with the ♠A and North trumps it with the ◇9.

Because East is also out of spades, he can win this trick by over-trumping with the ◇10.

4.

North
♠ 5
♡ J
◇ ---
♣ J

West
♠ K 3 2
♡ ---
◇ ---
♣ ---

East
♠ ---
♡ A Q
◇ ---
♣ K

South
♠ ---
♡ K 10
◇ ---
♣ Q

Clubs are trump!

East should win the trick with the ♡Q. Never win a trick with a higher card than is necessary. If East wins with the ♡A, South's ♡K becomes a winner.

East should now lead the ♣K. Remember, clubs are trump, and East can see that if he leads the ♡A North (dummy) will trump it with the ♣J. He prevents this by first "drawing" all outstanding trump with the ♣K.

East/West should win all three tricks.

COMING UP:

Basic Bidding

How to Suggest a Possible Trump Suit

Recommended time: 35 to 45 minutes

Dealer:

The person who deals the cards at the beginning of each hand. At the end of the hand, the deal passes to the person who is sitting to the dealer's left.

Clockwise:

To the left.

Everything in bridge is done in this direction, including the deal of the cards.

Trick:

After all four people have played a card in clockwise order, that group of four cards is called a trick.

The suits:

The four suits are spades (♠), hearts (♡), diamonds (♢) and clubs (♣).

Instant Glossary

Declarer:

The person who will play the hand.

Dummy:

The partner of the declarer. After the opening lead has been made, he exposes his hand face up on the table. The declarer will then play both hands.

Opening leader:

The person to the left of the declarer. He will lead the first card to begin the play. The opening lead is always made before the dummy is exposed.

Trump:

A designated suit, any card of which may win a trick if the person who holds it cannot follow suit to the trick in progress. A wild card.

Now that you know how bridge is played, you can see that determining your trump suit is crucial to the game.

Previously, you were allowed to look at dummy before choosing your longest suit as trump. Unfortunately, you must choose your trump suit before the dummy is laid down. The rules do not permit looking at your partner's hand and it is considered bad form to ask him, "Hey, how many hearts do you have?" Or "How good are your spades?"

Does this mean there is no practical way to find your best trump suit?

Of course not! Would the world's greatest game let you grope in the dark? Never!

Before the play of each hand, both partnerships engage in a form of communication called bidding. It is during this period that the declarer and the trump suit are chosen.

In order to understand precisely what bidding is, imagine you are at an auction; the auctioneer bangs his gavel and the action is underway. If you bid the highest, the lot is yours.

Bridge works the same way, except that you bid with a partner and the prize is the opportunity for your side to play the hand.

Both you and the opponents will usually be in the bidding and the auction can become fiercely competitive.

The side which bids the highest will play the hand.

Note:

The bidding which precedes the play is called an auction.

Any of the four players can enter the auction, and the side which bids the highest will play the hand.

Some people, wanting to play
every hand, bid with reckless
abandon. These people are
undesirable as partners, and they
soon find few players willing to
sit at their table.

Bidding is only half of the game.
Later on you will learn that how
high you bid dictates how many
tricks must be won in the play.
The penalty for failing to make
the required number more than
offsets your winning the auction.

You and your partner will speak
in a "foreign language" to assess
the trick-taking potential of the
two hands. This is called
bidding!

If you want to become a good
partner, learn to bid correctly.

We will begin by looking at
bidding in its most basic form.
The opponents will remain silent
until after the first four hours,
so just concentrate on understanding your partner.

Notes:

Explanation:

You and partner will attempt to find the longest suit between the two hands. What you are looking for is called a fit, and a fit is defined as any suit in which the partnership has a combined holding of at least eight cards.

Once you have a fit, you have an adequate trump suit. Some of the time you will have more than one fit and some of the time you will have no fit at all. The hands which have no common suit will usually be played in notrump.

Try to find your fit on the worksheets which follow.

North

♠ 9 5 3 2
♡ A J 8
♢ 7 6
♣ K Q 10 3

South

♠ 8 7 6 4
♡ K Q 3
♢ A 10 8
♣ A J 4

These two hands have a fit in spades. You will notice that a fit has nothing to do with high cards.

North

♠ J 10 8 7 5 4 3 2
♡ K J 6
♢ 6
♣ 5

South

♠ ---
♡ A 7 3 2
♢ K Q J 10 9
♣ K 8 6 2

These hands also have a fit, even though the eight spades are all in one hand. Any time the partnership holds eight cards in a common suit, it's a fit!

Find The Fit

Each of the following problems contain two hands, yours and your partner's. Circle the fit (or fits) between the two hands.

	You		Your Partner

1.
- ♠ A J 10 8
- ♡ 7 6
- ◇ A K Q
- ♣ J 10 9 8

1.
- ♠ 5 4 3 2
- ♡ Q J 9 8 5
- ◇ 10 9 8
- ♣ A

2.
- ♠ 6 5 4 3 2
- ♡ A
- ◇ A Q J 10
- ♣ K Q J

2.
- ♠ A K
- ♡ K 8 7 6 5 4 2
- ◇ 9 4 2
- ♣ 3

3.
- ♠ J 10 8 5 3 2
- ♡ A K J
- ◇ A K
- ♣ 3 2

3.
- ♠ A 7
- ♡ 10 8
- ◇ J 8 6 4 3 2
- ♣ J 10 9

4.
- ♠ K Q J 10
- ♡ 5 4 3 2
- ◇ A K Q J
- ♣ 7

4.
- ♠ A 8 7 4
- ♡ 9 8 7 6
- ◇ 10 9 8 7
- ♣ 5

5.
- ♠ K J
- ♡ A 5 4
- ◇ A Q
- ♣ J 10 9 8 7 6

5.
- ♠ 9 8 7 5 3 2
- ♡ K
- ◇ K J 8 6
- ♣ 5 3

Find The Fit

	You		Your Partner

6.

♠ A 6 4 2
♡ K J 10 8
◇ 10 9 8
♣ A K

6.

♠ K J
♡ Q 7 5
◇ A 2
♣ Q 7 5 4 3 2

7.

♠ 3 2
♡ A Q J 10 9 8
◇ A J 6 4
♣ Q

7.

♠ J 9 8 7 6 5 4
♡ K
◇ K Q
♣ J 3 2

8.

♠ K J 7 6 5 4
♡ A Q J
◇ A 2
♣ 9 8

8.

♠ A
♡ 10 9 8 5 3
◇ K J 7 6 4
♣ J 2

9.

♠ A K J 10
♡ K Q J 10
◇ J 8 6
♣ 6 4

9.

♠ 9 8 7 4 3 2
♡ 5 4 3 2
◇ A K
♣ 8

10.

♠ J 8 6 5 4 3 2
♡ Q
◇ A K Q
♣ K 7

10.

♠ 9
♡ 8 7 6 5 4 3 2
◇ J
♣ A Q J 10

Find The Fit
Answers:

The following suits should be circled:

1. Spades.

2. Hearts.

3. Spades and diamonds.

4. Spades, hearts and diamonds.

5. Spades and clubs.

6. Clubs.

7. Spades.

8. Hearts.

9. Spades and hearts.

10. Spades and hearts.

Explanation:

Once you know what a fit is, the next step is to discover if you and your partner have one. This is done through bidding, a mechanism which will allow you to suggest your long suits as possible trump suits.

But before you can begin to exchange information, you have to know something about the structure of bidding and the worth of the four suits.

Each suit has a certain value and you take this into consideration whenever you make a bid. Spades is the highest suit and then in descending order come hearts, diamonds and clubs, the lowest suit of all.

If someone bids hearts, the only suit you can outbid them with is spades. If they bid diamonds, both hearts and spades are higher. Every time you make a bid, it must be higher than the previous bid.

There are seven levels you can bid on, the first being the lowest and the seventh, the highest. A higher level always takes precedence over suit value. If the bid you have to beat is one spade (1♠) you can do so by bidding any suit on the second level. For example, two clubs (2♣) is higher than one spade (1♠).

Notrump and the four suits are ranked as follows, from the highest to the lowest:

Notrump (not a suit, but holds the highest rank on any given level)

Spades (♠)

Hearts (♡)

Diamonds (♢)

Clubs (♣)

Explanation:

The chart on the next page is called the apartment building principle. You bid just as if you were climbing from floor to floor.

Your building has seven floors (seven levels of bidding) and each floor has five steps. Notice that the highest step on each floor is called notrump. This is what you bid when you want to suggest playing the hand with no trump suit, simply highest card wins. Notrump is even higher than spades (♤), but for now, we will work with only the four suits.

Before going on, study the illustration and make sure you understand how to bid higher than the previous bid.

Notes:

The Apartment Building Principle

```
                    nt_____
                    ♠_____
7th floor           ♡_____
                    ◊_____
                    ♣_____

                    nt_____
                    ♠_____
6th floor           ♡_____
                    ◊_____
                    ♣_____

                    nt_____
                    ♠_____
5th floor           ♡_____
                    ◊_____
                    ♣_____

                    nt_____
                    ♠_____
4th floor           ♡_____
                    ◊_____
                    ♣_____

                    nt_____
                    ♠_____
3rd floor           ♡_____
                    ◊_____
                    ♣_____

                    nt_____
                    ♠_____
2nd floor           ♡_____
                    ◊_____
                    ♣_____

                    nt_____
                    ♠_____
1st floor           ♡_____
                    ◊_____
                    ♣_____
```

The good news:

You have just inherited an apartment building in mid-town Manhattan.

The bad news:

There is no elevator.

Therefore:

In order to get from floor to floor, you must climb up stairs.

Each floor has 5 steps, ♣'s, ◊'s, ♡'s, ♠'s and notrump. You can skip over steps on the way up, but NEVER go downstairs (backwards).

You must continue climbing until you find a resting place.

Explanation:

Now you can bid some hands. Assume that you and partner are the only two people at the table. Ordinarily, you would not be allowed to see his cards, but for now you should bid both hands to understand how bidding works.

Here are a few simple rules.

You and your partner will alternate bids, each suggesting a suit when it is your turn to speak.

No player is allowed more than one bid per turn.

Always bid your longest suit first, but each suit you bid must be at least four cards in length.

Never bid a suit on a higher level than necessary. For example, if your partner has bid one heart (1♡) and you want to mention spades, bid just one spade (1♠) because spades are higher than hearts and you can stay on the same level. If over your partner's bid of one heart (1♡) you want to suggest clubs, bid two clubs (2♣). This time you must go to the next highest level because clubs are lower than hearts.

If you have more than one four card suit, always bid the lowest one first. For example, if you have four hearts and four spades, start out by bidding one heart (1♡) because it is lower.

This is really very easy. Get your pencil ready, and I will prove it.

You hold this hand:

  ♠ K J 8 6 4
  ♡ A K
  ◇ J 6
  ♣ K 10 9 8

Which suit do you bid first?

    Bid spades.
    Always bid
    your longest
    suit first.

You hold this hand:

  ♠ A Q 8 6
  ♡ K
  ◇ K 4 3 2
  ♣ Q 6 4 3

Which suit do you bid first?

    Bid clubs.
    With more
    than one four
    card suit,
    always bid
    the lowest
    one first.

For convenience we will call you West, and your partner East, but we are going to bid both hands. West will make the opening bid (first bid) and from now on, all bids will be written in their abbreviated form.

West   East

♠ K Q 10 8   ♠ 7 4 3
♡ 6   ♡ K Q J 5
◇ Q 7 4 3   ◇ J 8 6 2
♣ A K 5 2   ♣ 10 9

As West, you should open by bidding 1♣. What you are really saying is, "Partner, I have at least four clubs, do we have a fit?"

East should respond by saying 1◇. "No, we don't have a fit in clubs, but I have at least four diamonds; how about that?"

Fit!
Now let East know.

West bids 2◇, confirming the fit by bidding East's suit at the next possible level.

Remember, partner cannot know you have a fit unless you tell him. For now (later there will be other options) acknowledge a fit by raising the suit to the next level and that will end the auction.

Do another one.

West   East

♠ J 10 9 8   ♠ K Q 3 2
♡ A K J 10   ♡ 8 4 2
◇ J   ◇ 10 9 7 5
♣ K 6 5 3   ♣ 7 4

Here is a way to write your bids in shorthand!

The easiest way to transcribe your bidding is to write the level (by number) followed by the first initial of the suit you are bidding.

For example, 2S means two spades. 5D stands for five diamonds; 3C is three clubs, and so on.

NT is the abbreviation for notrump. 1 NT means one notrump, etc.

West opens with 1♣ and East responds 1◊. Do they have a fit?

No, they don't! What should West bid now?

West bids 1♡ and East, still looking for a fit, bids 1♠.

What just happened?

Fit!

West acknowledges by bidding 2♠.

If you wanted to write this auction out, it would be done like this:

West		East		
1.	1C	1.	1D	
2.	1H	2.	1S	
3.	2S	3.	P	*

* This is something new. The "P" stands for pass. A pass is made whenever a player has nothing to say. It simply means that that player is passing his turn to bid. All auctions must end with a pass.

When four people are bidding, a player may pass on one turn and bid on another. However, as soon as three players in a row pass, the auction is over.

Bid this hand and write the auction:

West	East
♠ A J 5 4	♠ Q 9 8 3
♡ 10 9	♡ A 6 5 4
◊ A K Q J	◊ 8 7
♣ 9 7 5	♣ Q 10 8

West		East	
1.	___	1.	___
2.	___	2.	___
3.	___	3.	___

If you did it correctly, it should look like this:

West		East	
1.	1D	1.	1H
2.	1S	2.	2S
3.	P	3.	___

Did you remember to end the auction by passing?

Explanation:

You can rebid a suit on a future turn if it has more cards than you originally promised.

West	East
♠ 7 4	♠ 10 6 3
♡ A 5 2	♡ Q 4 3
◊ A 4 2	◊ Q J 7 5 3
♣ K Q J 9 8	♣ A 3

West		East	
1.	1C	1.	1D
2.	2C	2.	2D
3.	3D	3.	P

West rebids clubs, showing five or more, but East still has no fit. East rebids his own suit, diamonds, and West acknowledges. Pass ends the auction.

Each time you rebid a suit, your partner needs one less card to have a fit!

Yes, you can rebid a suit for the third time if you have more cards than you promised the second time.

Bid a new suit on the one level before rebidding your original suit on the two level. This gives your partner more information. You can always rebid your first suit later.

West	East
♠ A J 10 9	♠ Q 8 4 2
♡ A 2	♡ K 8 7 6 3
◊ K J 5 4 2	◊ 9 7
♣ J 6	♣ Q 9

West		East	
1.	1D	1.	1H
2.	1S	2.	2S
3.	P	3.	____

West bids 1♠ before repeating his diamonds and East acknowledges.

Try to keep the bidding on as low a level as possible. You should bid a suit on the one level before trying a different suit on the two level.

You hold:
- ♠ 8 6 5
- ♡ K Q 4 3
- ◊ A 7
- ♣ J 10 8 6

and hear your partner open 1◊. You should bid 1♡ and not 2♣, because you can bid hearts on a lower level than clubs.

Now bid these hands!

1.

West:

♠ Q J 10 8
♡ A Q J 10
♢ 8
♣ K J 4 3

East:

♠ K 7 4 3
♡ 8 5 3
♢ J 9 7 6
♣ A Q

West		East	
1.	_____	1.	_____
2.	_____	2.	_____
3.	_____	3.	_____
4.	_____	4.	_____
5.	_____	5.	_____
6.	_____	6.	_____

2.

West:

♠ A J 7
♡ K Q 10
♢ Q J 9 8 7
♣ J 2

Note: you can rebid a suit if you have more cards than originally promised.

East:

♠ K Q 10 6 4
♡ 8 4 3
♢ 10 6
♣ A 10 8

Note: you can rebid a suit if you have more cards than originally promised.

West		East	
1.	_____	1.	_____
2.	_____	2.	_____
3.	_____	3.	_____
4.	_____	4.	_____
5.	_____	5.	_____
6.	_____	6.	_____

3.

West:

♠ A
♡ K J 5 3
♢ 10 8 7
♣ A J 9 8 7

Note: bid a new suit on the one level before rebidding your original suit.

East:

♠ J 10 9 8
♡ 8 6 4
♢ A K J 5 4
♣ 3

Note: bid a new suit on the one level before rebidding your original suit.

West		East	
1.	_____	1.	_____
2.	_____	2.	_____
3.	_____	3.	_____
4.	_____	4.	_____
5.	_____	5.	_____
6.	_____	6.	_____

Answers:

1. **West**   **East**
   1. 1C   1. 1D
   2. 1H   2. 1S
   3. 2S   3. P

2. **West**   **East**
   1. 1D   1. 1S
   2. 2D   2. 2S
   3. 3S   3. P

3. **West**   **East**
   1. 1C   1. 1D
   2. 1H   2. 1S
   3. 2C   3. 2D
   4. 3D   4. P

Note: if you bid any of these
hands incorrectly, go
back and review the
explanations before
proceeding any
further.

Explanation:

You can bid a new suit on a higher level, but it must rank below your original suit.

West	East
♠ ---	♠ Q 9 8 5
♡ A J 8 7	♡ 6 3 2
◇ K Q J 10 9	◇ 8 4
♣ Q J 3 2	♣ A 10 8 7

West		East	
1.	1D	1.	1S
2.	2C	2.	3C
3.	P	3.	___

West could have rebid 2◇ (showing five) but his bid of 2♣ shows four clubs and also tells East that he has at least five diamonds. This is why. If West started out with only four diamonds and four clubs, he would have bid clubs first. Therefore, he must have more diamonds than clubs.

West also has four hearts, but hearts is above his original suit. As far as West knows, East cannot have four hearts because he bid 1♠. If East had both four hearts and four spades, he would have bid hearts first.

If you do not completely understand this, you will by the end of the fourth hour. For now, just remember the rule and bid accordingly.

Finally, when you are unable to show a new suit or rebid your original suit, you suggest notrump. When both partners are out of bids, you have a "fit" in notrump.

Here is how this works.

West	East
♠ A K J 8	♠ Q 7 4 3
♡ K J 10 3	♡ A 9 6 5
◇ 8	◇ K 7 6 3
♣ Q 4 3 2	♣ J

West		East	
1.	1C	1.	1D
2.	1H	2.	2H
3.	P	3.	___

You can see that West and East have two fits and that spades, their second suit, was never mentioned.

In general, do not look for a second fit after you have found one in another suit.

West		East	
♠ K Q J		♠ 10 9 6 4	
♡ A 8 7		♡ Q 6 3	
◊ J 8 5		◊ A K Q	
♣ K 10 9 7		♣ J 4 3	

	West		East
1.	1C	1.	1S
2.	1NT	2.	2NT
3.	P	3.	____

West bids 1NT because he has no other bid. East also has nothing else to say and acknowledges in notrump.

This is the end of the second section, but before you continue, bid the hands on the next page.

Bid these hands!

1.

West:

♠ K J
♡ K J 9 8 7
◇ A J
♣ Q 10 9 8

Note: bid a
new suit on the
two level (must
be below first
suit) before
rebidding your
original suit.

East:

♠ Q 5 4 3 2
♡ Q 10 2
◇ K 10 9 8
♣ A

Note: bid a
new suit on the
two level (must
be below first
suit) before
rebidding your
original suit.

West		East	
1.	_____	1.	_____
2.	_____	2.	_____
3.	_____	3.	_____
4.	_____	4.	_____
5.	_____	5.	_____
6.	_____	6.	_____

2.

West:

♠ A Q J
♡ J 8 5
◇ A 10 9 8
♣ Q 9 6

Note: when
you have no
available
bid, suggest
notrump.

East:

♠ K 3 2
♡ A K 4 3
◇ J 5 3
♣ 10 8 7

Note: when partner
has bid notrump and
you have no avail-
able bid, acknowledge
his notrump.

West		East	
1.	_____	1.	_____
2.	_____	2.	_____
3.	_____	3.	_____
4.	_____	4.	_____
5.	_____	5.	_____
6.	_____	6.	_____

3.

West:

♠ A J 10 9
♡ 3 2
◇ Q J 3
♣ A K 4 2

Note: when
partner has
bid notrump
and you have
no available
bid,
acknowledge
his notrump.

East:

♠ K 4 3
♡ 10 8 5
◇ A 10 9 5
♣ 6 5 3

Note: when you
have no available
bid, suggest
notrump.

West		East	
1.	_____	1.	_____
2.	_____	2.	_____
3.	_____	3.	_____
4.	_____	4.	_____
5.	_____	5.	_____
6.	_____	6.	_____

Answers:

1. **West**   **East**

    1. 1H*   1. 1S**
    2. 2C   2. 2D
    3. 2H   3. 3H
    4. P   4. ___

  * West bids hearts
     first because it's
     his longest suit.

 ** East bids spades
     for the same reason.

2. **West**   **East**

    1. 1D   1. 1H
    2. 1NT   2. 2NT
    3. P   3. ___

3. **West**   **East**

    1. 1C   1. 1D
    2. 1S   2. 1NT
    3. 2NT   3. P

Note: if you bid any of these
       hands incorrectly, go
       back and review the
       explanations before
       proceeding any
       further.

Questions:

1. Everything in bridge is played in what direction?

2. If East is the declarer, who is the dummy?

3. If South wins a trick, who leads the first card to the next trick?

4. What do you call the bidding which proceeds the play?

5. What is a fit?

6. Name the four suits in order, from the highest to the lowest.

7. Which is higher, 3◊ or 2♣?

8. Which is higher, 3♥ or 3NT?

9. If you have four clubs and four diamonds, which suit do you bid first?

10. If you have four clubs and five spades, which suit do you bid first?

11. What bid ends every auction?

Answers:

1. clockwise.

2. West.

3. South.

4. an auction.

5. eight cards held in a common suit between you and your partner.

6. spades, hearts, diamonds and clubs.

7. 3◊.

8. 3NT.

9. clubs.

10. spades (longest suit first).

11. pass.

Optional:

While you are waiting for the third section, you can play these hands, just for practice.

1. South is the declarer and there is no trump suit. South leads the ♠2.

    Who plays next?

    If West follows with the ♠4, what card should South play from dummy?

1.

<table>
<tr><td></td><td>North
♠ K 5
♡ ---
◊ 10
♣ ---</td><td></td></tr>
<tr><td>West
♠ A 4
♡ ---
◊ 6
♣ ---</td><td></td><td>East
♠ Q 10
♡ ---
◊ Q
♣ ---</td></tr>
<tr><td></td><td>South
♠ 7 3 2
♡ ---
◊ ---
♣ ---</td><td></td></tr>
</table>

2. North is the declarer and spades are trump.

    Who is the dummy?

    North leads the ♡4.

    Who plays next?

    How can North/South win both of the tricks?

2.

<table>
<tr><td></td><td>North
♠ K
♡ 4
◊ ---
♣ ---</td><td></td></tr>
<tr><td>West
♠ ---
♡ 3
◊ ---
♣ A</td><td></td><td>East
♠ ---
♡ A 10
◊ ---
♣ ---</td></tr>
<tr><td></td><td>South
♠ 10
♡ ---
◊ ---
♣ 5</td><td></td></tr>
</table>

Analysis:

1.

North

♠ K 5
♡ ---
♢ 10
♣ ---

West

♠ A 4
♡ ---
♢ 6
♣ ---

East

♠ Q 10
♡ ---
♢ Q
♣ ---

South

♠ 7 3 2
♡ ---
♢ ---
♣ ---

<u>There <u>is</u> <u>no</u> <u>trump</u> <u>suit</u></u>!

After South leads the ♠2, West will play next.

When West follows with the ♠4, South should play dummy's king. In a real game, South would not see West's cards, but he must hope that West and not East holds the ♠A. If East has it, South has no chance to win a trick.

Write the hand down on a piece of paper, exchanging the East and West hands, and you will see what I mean.

This is called leading toward a high card; more details will follow later.

2.

North

♠ K
♡ 4
♢ ---
♣ ---

West

♠ ---
♡ 3
♢ ---
♣ A

East

♠ ---
♡ A 10
♢ ---
♣ ---

South

♠ 10
♡ ---
♢ ---
♣ 5

<u>Spades</u> <u>are</u> <u>trump</u>!

If North is the declarer, South must be the dummy.

After North leads the ♡4, East will play next.

North must trump the ♡4 with dummy's ♠10. Then when dummy leads the ♠5, North will in the trick by trumping it with his ♠K.

3. West is the declarer
   and clubs are trump.

   What card should West
   play to the first trick?

   How about the second
   trick?

   If West plays correctly,
   how many tricks will
   East/West win?

3.

   North
   ♠ ---
   ♡ Q 2
   ♢ ---
   ♣ 10 8

   West   East
   ♠ A   ♠ Q
   ♡ A   ♡ 6 4
   ♢ ---   ♢ ---
   ♣ A K   ♣ 3

   South
   ♠ 8 7
   ♡ ---
   ♢ ---
   ♣ Q J

4. South is the declarer
   and there is no trump
   suit. South plays the
   ♠10.

   Who plays next?

   What card should West
   follow with?

   If West plays the ♠4,
   what card should South
   play from dummy?

4.

   North
   ♠ A Q
   ♡ ---
   ♢ ---
   ♣ ---

   West   East
   ♠ K 4   ♠ 6 3
   ♡ ---   ♡ ---
   ♢ ---   ♢ ---
   ♣ ---   ♣ ---

   South
   ♠ 10 8
   ♡ ---
   ♢ ---
   ♣ ---

Analysis:

3.

North
- ♠ ---
- ♡ Q 2
- ◇ ---
- ♣ 10 8

West
- ♠ A
- ♡ A
- ◇ ---
- ♣ A K

East
- ♠ Q
- ♡ 6 4
- ◇ ---
- ♣ 3

South
- ♠ 8 7
- ♡ ---
- ◇ ---
- ♣ Q J

Clubs are trump!

West should lead the ♣A to the first trick and the ♣K to the second. Naturally, if you led the ♣K first, that's still the right play.

When you have only high card winners left, it's a good idea not to let anyone trump them. If you led either the ♠A or the ♡A, one of the opponents would do just that.

You can prevent this by drawing their trump.

East/West will win all four tricks.

4.

North
- ♠ A Q
- ♡ ---
- ◇ ---
- ♣ ---

West
- ♠ K 4
- ♡ ---
- ◇ ---
- ♣ ---

East
- ♠ 6 3
- ♡ ---
- ◇ ---
- ♣ ---

South
- ♠ 10 8
- ♡ ---
- ◇ ---
- ♣ ---

There is no trump suit!

After South leads the ♠10, West will play next.

West should follow with the ♠4 because he can see the ♠A and ♠Q in the dummy. If he plays his king, he knows the ace will capture it, and South will have two sure tricks.

South should play dummy's queen. Declarer does not know that West has the king, but playing the queen is his only chance to win two tricks.* This is called a finesse, and will be explained in more detail later.

*Note, if after leading the ♠10 South goes up with dummy's ace, he will lose a trick to the king no matter who has it.

Point Count

Basic Rules for Bidding

Recommended time: 35 to 45 minutes

As you do the final sections, it's important that you don't spend too much time on any one part.

Don't try to memorize anything!

Just read through each section and follow along with the explanations.

You should work your way through most of these pages in only slightly more time than it would take for a normal reading.

In bridge, you need a certain number of points to open and continue the bidding.

The worth of your hand is determined by adding its high card points. An ace counts 4 points, a king 3 points, a queen is 2 points and a jack 1 point.

You need at least 13 points to open the bidding. If your partner has opened, you are called the responder and need at least 6 points to respond to his opening bid.

There are other factors which add or subtract value from your hand, but for now we will work only with high card points. If you have 13 points you must open, and with 6 points, you must respond. Otherwise, pass!

The dealer always has the first bid, but if he lacks enough points to open, he passes his turn to the player at his left. The bidding then proceeds until someone can open. If no one does, the cards are reshuffled and dealt over.

Once someone has opened, each player bids or passes in turn until the auction is over.

There are a total of 40 high card points in a deck of cards, 10 in each suit. The ace, king, queen, jack and ten of each suit are called honor cards. The ten is an honor even though it gets no points.

You and partner will still suggest your suits back and forth, only now you need a minimum number of points to enter the bidding.

Count your points of the page which follows.

Each deck contains 40 high card points.

```
    ace - 4 pts.
    king - 3 pts.
    queen - 2 pts.
    jack - 1 pt.
```

You need 13 points to open the bidding...

and 6 points to respond to your partner's opening bid.

You hold this hand:

```
    ♠ K Q J 6
    ♡ A J 7 5
    ◇ K Q 3 2
    ♣ 10
```

Count your points.

You have 16. Here's how you should count it.

♠	♡	◇	♣
K (3)	A (4)	K (3)	10
Q (2)	J (1)	Q (2)	
J (1)	7	3	
6	5	2	

If you add your points by suits, you have 6 in spades, 5 in hearts and diamonds, and none in clubs. This makes a total of 16 points.

Count your points:

1.   ♠ A 10 9 8
      ♡ J 6 4 3
      ◊ A K J
      ♣ 10 9 8

_____

2.   ♠ K J 7 5
      ♡ Q J 10
      ◊ A 3 2
      ♣ 7 5 3

_____

3.   ♠ A J 10 8 6
      ♡ J 10 5 3
      ◊ 9
      ♣ Q 10 6

_____

4.   ♠ A K Q J
      ♡ 8 4 3
      ◊ J 10
      ♣ A K Q J

_____

5.   ♠ A Q 6 5 4
      ♡ K 6
      ◊ A 10 9 8
      ♣ A K

_____

6.   ♠ K 10 7 6
      ♡ Q J 8 7 5
      ◊ J 3 2
      ♣ 10

_____

Now, circle those hands which qualify only for a response.

Answers: 1. 13 points.
            2. 11 points.
            3. 8 points.
            4. 21 points.
            5. 20 points.
            6. 7 points.

Hands numbered 2, 3 and 6 should be circled as they contain too few points to open, but enough to respond.

Explanation:

Spades and hearts (the higher suits) are called the major suits, while diamonds and clubs (the lower suits) are called the minor suits.

In order to open the bidding with a major suit (1♡ or 1♠) you must have at least 5 cards in it. If your partner shows a fit, he promises a minimum of 3-card support.

Remember, this rule applies only to an opening bid. If you are responding or bidding on your second turn (after opening) you can always bid a 4 card major.

West (14)	East (8)
♠ J 9 8 5 4	♠ Q 10 6
♡ A K Q	♡ J 8 4 3
◇ K J 9	◇ A 5 4 2
♣ 8 6	♣ J 10

1.	1S		1.	2S
2.	P		2.	

West opens 1♠ because he has 13 or more points and at least 5 spades. Notice that his high cards are not necessarily in the suit he bids. East, with at least 6 points and 3 spades, acknowledges a fit by raising one level.

When you rebid a major suit after opening it, you promise at least 6 cards in length. Responder needs 2-card support to show a fit.

West (13)	East (10)
♠ J 7	♠ A Q 10 4
♡ A J 9 8 7 3	♡ K 2
◇ Q 10 8	◇ J 9 4 3
♣ A J	♣ 10 5 4

Note:

Counting points is strictly mechanical, and the more you practice it, the quicker you will do it. But if you tried to count out every remaining hand, you would spend all your time counting.

So from now on, the number of points in each hand will be noted in parentheses ( ) after the titles, West and East.

West (13)	East (6)
♠ A Q 9 6 3	♠ K 8 5 4
♡ A K	♡ Q 8 5 4
◇ 10 8 5	◇ J 9 7
♣ 6 4 3	♣ 8 7

As you can see, West has 13 points and East, 6.

Do not count points!

Use the totals which are provided. Later you can practice on hands which appeared earlier.

1.	1H		1.	1S
2.	2H		2.	3H
3.	P		3.	___

West opens 1♡ and East, not knowing yet that he has a fit, responds 1♠. West promises at least 6 hearts by rebidding them, allowing East to show a fit.

In order to open the bidding with a minor suit (1♣ or 1◊) you promise as few as 3 cards in it. If your partner shows a fit, he must have 5-card support.

Again, this applies only to an opening bid.

West (14)

♠ A 4 3 2
♡ A J 5 3
◊ A 3
♣ J 6 4

East (8)

♠ K Q 10
♡ 8 6 4
◊ J 5
♣ Q 10 8 7 3

1.	1C		1.	2C
2.	P		2.	___

West cannot open 1♡ or 1♠ because he does not have 5 of them. He must, therefore, open in a minor. His longest is 3 cards so he opens 1♣. East could not show a fit unless he had at least 5 clubs.

When you rebid a minor suit after opening it, you promise at least 5 cards in length.

West (14)

♠ A K J
♡ J 10 8
◊ K Q 10 9 5
♣ 3 2

East (7)

♠ 7 6 5
♡ A 9 7 3
◊ J 6 2
♣ Q 10 8

When you open a major suit, you promise at least 5 cards in length!

West (14)

♠ A J 9 8 6
♡ K J 8
◊ Q J 9
♣ Q 3

East (10)

♠ K Q 10
♡ A 4
◊ 8 5 4 3
♣ J 10 9 8

West opens 1♠ and East needs only 3-card support to show a fit.

When you open a minor suit, you promise only 3 cards in length!

West (14)

♠ K Q J 10
♡ K 10 8 5
◊ A J 10
♣ 7 4

East (8)

♠ 9 8 5
♡ A 4 3
◊ Q 9 6 4 3
♣ Q 8

West opens 1◊ (he does not have a 5 card major) and East must have 5-card support to show a fit.

1.	1D		1.	1H
2.	2D		2.	3D
3.	P		3.	___

West opens 1◊ and East, not knowing yet that he has a fit, responds 1♡. West promises at least 5 diamonds by rebidding them, allowing East to show a fit.

All other rules remain the same, so bid the hands on the pages which follow.

Remember, don't spend time counting points. Totals for each hand are given in parentheses ( ) after the titles, West and East.

A quick review:

You must have at least 13 points to open the bidding and 6 points to respond. Otherwise, pass!

You need a minimum of 5 cards in a major and 3 in a minor in order to open it.

After opening a major suit, a rebid of that same suit promises at least 6 cards. A rebid of a minor promises at least 5 cards.

All new suits bid by responder and opener (after the opening bid) still promise only 4 cards in length.

Bid a new suit on the one level before rebidding your original suit on the two level.

Finally, when you have no available bid, suggest notrump!

Bid these hands!

1.

West: (14)

♠ A Q 10 9
♡ A J 7
◇ J 10 8 6 4
♣ Q

Note: bid a new suit on the one level before rebidding your original suit.

East: (8)

♠ K 8 4
♡ 10 8 5 3 2
◇ A 3
♣ J 10 3

Note: you can rebid a suit if you have more cards than originally promised.

1. ____	1. ____
2. ____	2. ____
3. ____	3. ____
4. ____	4. ____
5. ____	5. ____
6. ____	6. ____

2.

West: (8)

♠ K Q 8 4
♡ Q 3 2
◇ 9 8 5 4
♣ J 10

East: (14)

♠ J 3
♡ A K J 10 8
◇ A J 3
♣ 9 8 5

Note: you must have at least 5 cards in a major suit in order to open it.

1. ____	1. ____
2. ____	2. ____
3. ____	3. ____
4. ____	4. ____
5. ____	5. ____
6. ____	6. ____

3.

West: (16)

♠ K J 9 8
♡ A Q
◇ 3 2
♣ A Q 10 8 6

East: (9)

♠ Q 10 4
♡ 8 5 3 2
◇ A Q J
♣ 5 4 2

Note: when you have no available bid, suggest notrump.

1. ____	1. ____
2. ____	2. ____
3. ____	3. ____
4. ____	4. ____
5. ____	5. ____
6. ____	6. ____

Answers:

The page number which explains each bid is now given in parentheses ( ). If you missed any of the bidding, go back and review the explanations before proceeding any further.

Page numbers will continue to be given on all "bid these hands" answer sheets, so you can determine why you missed a particular answer.

1. West   East

    1.   1D   (47)   1.   1H   (27)
    2.   1S   (30)   2.   2H   (30)
    3.   3H   (30)   3.   P

After bidding 1♦, West is prepared to rebid his diamonds, but East rebids his hearts, promising at least five of them. West now has a fit and shows it. In general, do not look for two fits once you find one.

2. West   East

    1.   P   (44)   1.   1H   (46)
    2.   2H   (46)   2.   P

West cannot open because he lacks 13 points. After East opens, however, he has enough to respond.

3. West   East

    1.   1C   (47)   1.   1H   (27)
    2.   1S   (30)   2.   1NT (33)
    3.   2C   (47)   3.   3C   (48)
    4.   P   4.

West bids a new suit (spades) on the one level before rebidding his clubs on the two level. As soon as West does rebid his clubs, East confirms the fit.

Explanation:

With two 4 card minors, always open 1♣, regardless of honor card strength.

West (14)   East (11)

♠ J 5   ♠ A 10 9 3
♡ A K 8   ♡ 6 4 3
◇ K J 9 7   ◇ Q 10 2
♣ Q 10 5 4   ♣ A J 9

1. __1C__   1. __1S__
2. __1NT__   2. __2NT__
3. __P__   3. _____

With 4 clubs and 4 diamonds, West opens 1♣. After East responds 1♠, West cannot rebid 2◇, because diamonds are not below his origianl suit, clubs.

Remember, if you bid a new suit on a higher level, it must be below your original suit.

Therefore, West has no available rebid, so he suggests notrump and East confirms.

With two 3 card minors, open the one with better high cards.

West (13)   East (9)

♠ Q 10 8   ♠ 9 7 4
♡ A Q 10 9   ♡ 6 5 3
◇ K Q 10   ◇ A 5 4 3 2
♣ 10 8 7   ♣ A J

1. __1D__   1. __2D__
2. __P__   2. _____

West has two 3 card minors, but diamonds are better in terms of high cards. He opens 1◇ and East shows a fit.

Notes:

With two 5 (or 6) card suits,
always open the higher one first,
regardless of high card strength.

West (14)		East (9)	
♠	A 2	♠	Q 10 9 8 7
♡	K Q J 7 5	♡	10 2
◊	A 10 8 6 4	◊	K 7 2
♣	4	♣	K J 9

	West		East
1.	1H	1.	1S
2.	2D	2.	2S
3.	3D	3.	4D
4.	P	4.	

With two 5 card suits, West opens
the higher one by bidding 1♡.
East responds 1♠ and West bids
2◊. Remember, opener's second
bid promises only 4-card length,
so East does not know about the
fit. When West rebids the
diamonds, he shows at least 5,
and now East knows.

The same rule also applies to the
responder. After your partner
has opened, with two 5 (or 6)
card suits, always bid the
higher one first.

West (15)		East (8)	
♠	A K Q 2	♠	10 3
♡	K Q 8	♡	10 9 7 5 4
◊	10 8	◊	K Q J 6 3
♣	J 6 5 3	♣	Q

	West		East
1.	1C	1.	1H
2.	1S	2.	2D
3.	2H	3.	P

East responds 1♡ first, and shows
his diamonds later. If East had
only 4 diamonds and also only 4
hearts, his first response would
have been 1◊ and not 1♡. By
bidding hearts first, he promised
more cards in hearts than in
diamonds. Therefore, West knows

Notes:

that East has at least 5 hearts, and he shows a fit.

Remember, always bid your longest suit first.

Now, bid the hands which follow.

A quick review:

As opener:

With two 4 card minors, always open 1♣.

With two 3 card minors, open the one with better high cards.

With two 5 (or 6) card suits, always bid the higher one first.

With no available rebid, suggest notrump.

As responder:

Always bid your longest suit first.

With two 5 (or 6) card suits, always bid the higher one first.

With no available bid, suggest notrump.

Bid these hands!

1.

West: (15)

♠ K J 6
♡ A K
♢ Q J 9 8
♣ J 6 4 2

Note: with two 4 card minors, always open 1♣.

1. _____	1. _____
2. _____	2. _____
3. _____	3. _____
4. _____	4. _____
5. _____	5. _____
6. _____	6. _____

East: (9)

♠ A 10 9 8 7
♡ J 10 4 3
♢ A 2
♣ 10 3

Note: bid a new suit on the two level (must be below first suit) before rebidding your original suit.

2.

West: (15)

♠ 8 6 4 3 2
♡ A K Q J 10
♢ A J
♣ 8

Note: with two 5 (or 6) card suits, always bid the higher one first.

1. _____	1. _____
2. _____	2. _____
3. _____	3. _____
4. _____	4. _____
5. _____	5. _____
6. _____	6. _____

East: (8)

♠ Q 7 5
♡ 8
♢ K Q 10 9
♣ J 7 4 3 2

3.

West: (14)

♠ 10 8 6
♡ Q 10 8 4
♢ K Q 10
♣ A Q J

Note: with two 3 card minors, open the one with better high cards.

1. _____	1. _____
2. _____	2. _____
3. _____	3. _____
4. _____	4. _____
5. _____	5. _____
6. _____	6. _____

East: (4)

♠ A 4 3
♡ 9 7
♢ 8 4 2
♣ 10 9 8 7 6

Answers:

1. **West**   **East**

    1.   <u>1C</u> (51)   1.   <u>1S</u> (27)
    2. <u>1NT</u> (33)   2.   <u>2H</u> (33)
    3.   <u>2S</u> (33)   3.   <u>P</u>

When East responds 1♠, he promises only 4 cards, so
West is unaware of the fit. After East rebids 2♡, he
shows 5 spades, and West confirms the fit.

Remember, if East had only 4 spades and 4 hearts, he
would have bid hearts first. Because he bid 1♠ first,
he must have more spades than hearts.

2. **West**   **East**

    1.   <u>1S</u> (46)   1.   <u>2S</u> (46)
    2.   <u>P</u>   2.   <u>   </u>

3. **West**   **East**

    1.   <u>1C</u> (47)   1.   <u>P</u> (44)

Yes, East does have a fit, but he lacks the 6 points
necessary to give a response.

Bid these hands!

4.

West: (10)

♠ K J 2
♡ A J 8 6
♢ 10 7 6
♣ J 10 9

East: (13)

♠ Q 6 4
♡ K 7 3
♢ K Q 9 8 4
♣ K 3

Note: a rebid of a minor suit (after opening it) promises at least 5 cards in length.

	West		East
1.	_____	1.	_____
2.	_____	2.	_____
3.	_____	3.	_____
4.	_____	4.	_____
5.	_____	5.	_____
6.	_____	6.	_____

5.

West: (14)

♠ K 7
♡ 8 4 3
♢ A 5 3 2
♣ A Q J 4

Note: with two 4 card minors, always open 1♣.

East: (9)

♠ A J 10 3 2
♡ J
♢ K 10 8 6 4
♣ 6 2

Note: with two 5 (or 6) card suits, always bid the higher one first.

	West		East
1.	_____	1.	_____
2.	_____	2.	_____
3.	_____	3.	_____
4.	_____	4.	_____
5.	_____	5.	_____
6.	_____	6.	_____

6.

West: (14)

♠ K Q 5
♡ A 10 9 8 7 6 4
♢ K Q
♣ 10

Note: after opening a major, a rebid of that same suit promises at least 6 cards in length.

East: (7)

♠ J 9 8 6 4 3 2
♡ ---
♢ J 8 3
♣ K Q 7

Note: when responder rebids his original suit, it promises at least 5 cards in length.

	West		East
1.	_____	1.	_____
2.	_____	2.	_____
3.	_____	3.	_____
4.	_____	4.	_____
5.	_____	5.	_____
6.	_____	6.	_____

Answers:

4. West   East

    1.   P   (44)   1.   1D (47)
    2.   1H (27)   2.   2D (47)
    3.   3D (47)   3.   P

West does not have enough points to open so he passes.
When East rebids his diamonds, it shows at least 5 cards,
so West confirms the fit.

5. West   East

    1.   1C (51)   1.   1S (52)
    2.   1NT (33)   2.   2D (53)
    3.   3D (28)   3.   P

After East responds 1♠, West has no available bid, so
he suggest notrump. Remember, West cannot bid diamonds
because it is above his original suit. However, when
East shows at least 4 diamonds by bidding them at his
second turn, West acknowledges the fit.

6. West   East

    1.   1H (46)   1.   1S (27)
    2.   2H (46)   2.   2S (30)
    3.   3S (30)   3.   P

When East rebids his spades, West shows a fit even
though he has 7 hearts. If he did not have a fit, he
could bid his hearts a third time, because he has more
than he promised the second time.

COMING UP:

More on Basic Bidding

Contracts, Games and Slams

Recommended time: 30 to 40 minutes

Explanation:

When the responder's first bid is a new suit on the two level, he promises at least 5 cards in length and a minimum of 10 points.

West (14)   East (10)

♠ K J 9 5 3   ♠ Q 2
♡ A 4 3   ♡ Q J 9 8 5
◊ Q J 10   ◊ K 8 4
♣ K 3   ♣ Q 8 7

1. 1S   1. 2H
2. 3H   2. P

After West opens 1♠, East responds 2♡. West knows East must have at least 5 hearts (and 10 points) so he shows a fit.

Remember, this rule applies only to the responder's first bid.

The responder should never bid a new suit on the two level when he can bid it on the one level.

West (14)   East (10)

♠ K J 4   ♠ Q 2
♡ A 4 3   ♡ Q J 9 8 5
◊ Q J 5   ◊ K 8 4
♣ K 10 9 6   ♣ Q 8 7

1. 1C   1. 1H
2. 1NT   2. 2H
3. 3H   3. P

Even though East has 5 hearts and 10 or more points, his first bid is 1♡, because he can bid his suit on the one level. After he rebids hearts, West knows about the fit.

Remember, when responder's first bid is a new suit on the two level, he not only promises 5 cards, he guarantees 10 or more points.

West (15)   East (8)

♠ Q 10 9   ♠ K 3 2
♡ A K J 10 8   ♡ 6 4
◊ A 10   ◊ K 8 6 5 4
♣ J 5 3   ♣ Q 10 8

1. 1H   1. 1NT
2. 2NT   2. P

East has 5 diamonds, but lacks 10 points, so he can't bid 2◊. Therefore, he has no available bid and suggests notrump.

Bid these hands!

1.

West: (14)

♠ 10 9 7 5 3
♡ A K J
♢ K Q 10
♣ J 6

East: (11)

♠ A J
♡ Q 10 5 4 3 2
♢ J 8 4
♣ K 4

1. _____	1. _____
2. _____	2. _____
3. _____	3. _____
4. _____	4. _____
5. _____	5. _____
6. _____	6. _____

Note: when responder's first bid is a new suit on the two level, he promises 5 cards and 10 or more points.

2.

West: (11)

♠ K Q J 9 7
♡ 6 4 2
♢ A J 4
♣ 10 3

Note: responder never bids a new suit on the two level when he can bid it on the one level.

East: (14)

♠ 6 5 2
♡ K J 3
♢ 3 2
♣ A K Q J 4

1. _____	1. _____
2. _____	2. _____
3. _____	3. _____
4. _____	4. _____
5. _____	5. _____
6. _____	6. _____

3.

West: (14)

♠ J 7 6 5
♡ A K Q 4 3
♢ A 10
♣ 6 5

East: (7)

♠ K Q 2
♡ 10 5
♢ J 8 6
♣ J 10 9 8 4

1. _____	1. _____
2. _____	2. _____
3. _____	3. _____
4. _____	4. _____
5. _____	5. _____
6. _____	6. _____

Note: responder must have 10 or more points to bid a new suit on the two level for his first bid.

1. <u>West</u>   <u>East</u>

    1. <u>1S</u> (46)   1. <u>2H</u> (59)
    2. <u>3H</u> (59)   2. <u>P</u>

East meets all requirements, so his first bid is a new suit on the two level. West, knowing that East must have at least 5 hearts, confirms the fit.

2. <u>West</u>   <u>East</u>

    1. <u>P</u>   (44)   1. <u>1C</u> (47)
    2. <u>1S</u> (59)   2. <u>2C</u> (47)
    3. <u>2S</u> (30)   3. <u>3S</u> (30)
    4. <u>P</u>   4. <u> </u>

West cannot open because he lacks 13 points. East opens 1♣ and though West meets all requirements to bid a new suit on the two level, he bids only 1♠, because he can bid it on the one level.

Never bid a suit on the two level if you can bid it on the one level.

3. <u>West</u>   <u>East</u>

    1. <u>1H</u> (46)   1. <u>1NT</u> (33)
    2. <u>2NT</u> (33)   2. <u>P</u>

East cannot bid 2♣ because he does not have 10 points. Having no available bid, he suggests notrump and West confirms.

Notice that West cannot bid 2♣ because spades are above his original suit.

Questions:

1. How many points are required to open the bidding?

2. How many to respond?

3. How many points is a king worth?

4. How many points is a jack worth?

5. How many high card points are in a deck of cards?

6. Each suit has 5 honor cards. What are they?

7. What are the major suits?

8. How many cards (length) are needed to open a major suit?

9. After opening a major suit, how many cards are needed to rebid it?

10. What are the minor suits?

11. With two 4 card minors, which one should you open?

12. With two 3 card minors, which one should you open?

13. After opening a minor suit, how many cards are needed to rebid it?

14. As opener or responder, if you hold two 5 (or 6) card suits, which one do you bid first?

15. If responder's first bid is a new suit on the two level, exactly what does he promise his partner?

Answers:

1. 13.

2. 6.

3. 3.

4. 1.

5. 40.

6. the ace, king, queen, jack and ten.

7. hearts and spades.

8. at least 5.

9. at least 6.

10. clubs and diamonds.

11. clubs.

12. the one with better high cards.

13. at least 5.

14. always bid the higher one first.

15. at least 5 cards in his suit and 10 or more points.

Explanation:

Only one person from the declaring side will play the hand. The declarer is always the player who first declares the suit (or notrump) which is designated in the final bid.

West (14)

♠ K J 9 8 7
♡ A K
♢ Q 10 8
♣ J 9 7

East (8)

♠ A Q 10 6
♡ Q 5 4
♢ 7 6 2
♣ 8 5 3

| 1. | 1S |
| 2. | P |

| 1. | 2S |
| 2. | ___ |

The hand will be played with spades as trump. As West was the first person who declared spades, he is the declarer. East will be the dummy.

The number of tricks you must win in the play will be determined by how high you bid.

The formula works like this:

The declaring side always starts out with a handicap of six tricks. This is called "book." You must make your book, plus the same number of tricks as the level you stopped on.

For example, if the final bid is 4♡, you have to win ten (or more) tricks to get credit for your bidding. The first six are your book, while the extra four correspond to the level you stopped on.

If the final bid is 5♢, you must win at least 11 tricks. Book plus five.

The final bid (outside of pass) is called a contract, because you have contracted to win a certain number of tricks.

Explanation:

The auction may end on any one of seven levels. The higher the level, the more difficult it is to make your contract.

The best way to judge how high to bid is through point count.

Experience has proven that a given number of points between the two hands almost always produces a certain number of tricks.

During the final chapters, you will add your points to partner's, but first, you must know what you're looking for.

In bridge, a huge bonus is given for bidding to certain levels, if you can make the required number of tricks in the play.

These bonus levels are called games and slams.

Games are bid on the third, fourth and fifth level, depending on whether you decide to play in notrump or one of the four suits.

For example, if you are going to play in notrump, the third level is a game. If you bid 3NT, you must win at least 9 tricks in the play to receive your bonus.

The major suit games are 4♡ and 4♤. They are bid one level higher than notrump and require a minimum of 10 tricks in the play.

Notes:

Minor suit games (5♣ and 5♦) are harder to make because they are bid on the fifth level. This means you must win 11 or more tricks to score your bonus.

The partnership usually needs a minimum of 26 points between the combined hands to make game in either notrump or a major suit.

But you need at least 30 points to contract for game in a minor.

Due to a quirk in scoring you receive no extra credit for bidding past game levels until you reach the sixth or seventh level.

Therefore, it would be unwise to reach a contract like 4NT or 5♠. These contracts are one level higher than game and one trick harder to make. Even if you do make them, your bonus will be the same as if you had stopped at 3NT or 4♠.

The reward for bidding and making a game is large enough that the partnership should bid one whenever they hold the required number of points.

You won't always make your game, but if you hold enough points you should always bid it.

Conversely, if you lack the points for game you should play on as low a level as possible.

Remember, the higher you bid, the more tricks you must win in the play. Good bidders try to end the auction quickly, upon learning that there is little chance for game.

Notes:

In order to contract for a game bonus, the partnership should usually hold a certain number of points.

<u>3NT</u> a 9 trick game.	at least <u>26</u> points between the combined hands.
<u>4♡</u> or <u>4♠</u> a 10 trick game.	at least <u>26</u> points between the combined hands.
<u>5♣</u> or <u>5♢</u> an 11 trick game.	at least <u>30</u> points between the combined hands.

Explanation:

Slams are bid on the sixth or seventh level and pay a larger bonus than games.

Contracts on the sixth level are called small slams or simply slams, while contracts which reach the seventh level are always called grand slams.

Regardless of your trump suit (or notrump) six and seven level contracts are always slams. 6♣ is a slam as well as 6♠ and 6NT. All slams pay the same bonus.

These are extremely difficult contracts to make. The partner-ship usually needs at least 33 points for a slam, and at least 37 points for a grand slam.

For this reason, slams are rarely bid and slam bidding will not be covered until after the fourth hour.

Notes:

Questions:

1. What is a contract?

2. What is book and how does it affect the declaring side?

3. How many tricks must you win to make the following contracts?

    1NT _____

    2♣ _____

    4◊ _____

    7♣ _____

4. How do you determine who will be the declarer?

5. In the auction given below, who is the declarer?

West		East	
1.	1D	1.	1S
2.	2S	2.	_____

6. What contract is considered a game in notrump?

7. What are the two major suit game contracts?

8. What are the two minor suit game contracts?

9. What is the minimum number of points the partnership should hold to contract for game in notrump or a major suit?

10. How many points for game in a minor suit?

Answers:

1. the final bid; designates the number of tricks which must be made.

2. a six trick handicap given to the declaring side; add book to final level reached to determine how many tricks must be won.

3. 1NT: 7, 2♣: 8, 4◊: 10 and 7♣: 13.

4. it's the first person who declares the suit (or notrump) designated in the final bid.

5. East.

6. 3NT.

7. 4♡ and 4♣.

8. 5♣ and 5◊.

9. 26 points.

10. 30 points.

Optional:

Play these hands! *NO!*

From now on South will be the declarer on all play problems.

1. South is the declarer and there is no trump suit.

    South leads the ♡3 and West follows with the ♡8.

    What card should South play from dummy, and why?

1.

North

♠ ---
♡ Q 5
♢ ---
♣ ---

West

♠ ---
♡ K 8
♢ ---
♣ ---

East

♠ ---
♡ J 10
♢ ---
♣ ---

South

♠ ---
♡ 3 2
♢ ---
♣ ---

2. South is the declarer and hearts are trump.

    What card should South lead to the next trick? Why?

    If South plays correctly, how many tricks will North/South win?

2.

North

♠ ---
♡ 10
♢ Q 5
♣ ---

West

♠ ---
♡ J
♢ K 8
♣ ---

East

♠ 10 2
♡ 9
♢ ---
♣ ---

South

♠ ---
♡ K
♢ 3 2
♣ ---

Analysis:

1.

North
- ♠ ---
- ♡ Q 5
- ◊ ---
- ♣ ---

West
- ♠ ---
- ♡ K 8
- ◊ ---
- ♣ ---

East
- ♠ ---
- ♡ J 10
- ◊ ---
- ♣ ---

South
- ♠ ---
- ♡ 3 2
- ◊ ---
- ♣ ---

<u>There <u>is</u> <u>no</u> <u>trump</u> suit</u>!

South should go right up with dummy's queen.

In a real game, South would not know that West holds the ♡K, but if East has it, then dummy's queen will never score a trick.

Exchange the West and East hands and try and win a trick with dummy's queen. It cannot be done.

One of the first principles regarding good bridge play is that you must lead up to your high cards.

More on this later.

2.

North
- ♠ ---
- ♡ 10
- ◊ Q 5
- ♣ ---

West
- ♠ ---
- ♡ J
- ◊ K 8
- ♣ ---

East
- ♠ 10 2
- ♡ 9
- ◊ ---
- ♣ ---

South
- ♠ ---
- ♡ K
- ◊ 3 2
- ♣ ---

<u>Hearts</u> <u>are</u> <u>trump</u>!

South should lead the ♡K, drawing the opponents' trumps in the process.

South wants to lead the ◊3 toward his high card (◊Q) in dummy. But if he does this right away, he will never score his ◊Q because East will trump it. East will return a spade and West will make his ♡J whether South trumps with the ♡K or not.

If South draws trump, North/South will win 2 of 3 tricks.

3. South is the declarer and clubs are trump.

What card should South lead to the first trick? Why?

If South plays correctly, how many tricks will North/South win?

3.

        North
        ♠ ---
        ♡ ---
        ♢ 3 2
        ♣ A

West   East
♠ ---   ♠ ---
♡ ---   ♡ ---
♢ J 10 9   ♢ K 8 7
♣ ---   ♣ ---

        South
        ♠ ---
        ♡ ---
        ♢ Q 5
        ♣ 10

4. South is the declarer and there is no trump suit. South leads the ♢2.

What card should West follow with? Why?

If West plays the ♢7, what card should South play from dummy?

4.

        North
        ♠ ---
        ♡ ---
        ♢ A K J
        ♣ ---

West   East
♠ ---   ♠ ---
♡ ---   ♡ ---
♢ Q 8 7   ♢ 10 9 5
♣ ---   ♣ ---

        South
        ♠ ---
        ♡ ---
        ♢ 4 3 2
        ♣ ---

Analysis:

3.

North

♠ ---
♡ ---
♢ 3 2
♣ A

West

♠ ---
♡ ---
♢ J 10 9
♣ ---

East

♠ ---
♡ ---
♢ K 8 7
♣ ---

South

♠ ---
♡ ---
♢ Q 5
♣ 10

Clubs are trump!

South should lead the ♣10 to the first trick. West and East will shed diamonds as dummy's ♣A wins the trick.

This time the opponents have no trump, so why is South playing trump? Because that is the only way he can get to the dummy!

He wants to lead dummy's ♢3 toward the high card (♢Q) in his hand. The only way South can score his ♢Q is to lead the first diamond from dummy. The only way to get to the dummy is through the ♣A.

The fact that clubs are trump is irrelevant.

4.

North

♠ ---
♡ ---
♢ A K J
♣ ---

West

♠ ---
♡ ---
♢ Q 8 7
♣ ---

East

♠ ---
♡ ---
♢ 10 9 5
♣ ---

South

♠ ---
♡ ---
♢ 4 3 2
♣ ---

There is no trump suit!

West had better follow with a low diamond. He can see if he plays the ♢Q, he will lose it for sure, and dummy's ♢J will be an extra trick for declarer.

West does follow with the ♢7, but South can counter this fine defensive move by playing dummy's jack.

South is taking a chance that West has the ♢Q. If so, dummy's jack will win the trick. Only the ♢Q can beat the jack, and if East does not have it, he cannot win the trick.

This is called a finesse. More on this later.

COMING UP:

How High to Bid

How to Show Point Count

Recommended time: 45 to 55 minutes

| Auction: | A collective term used to describe the bidding which always proceeds the play. |

| Fit: | Whenever you and partner hold eight cards or more in a common suit, it's a fit. |

| Major suits: | The two higher suits, hearts and spades. The suits of most importance. |

| Minor suits: | The two lower suits, clubs and diamonds. |

| Honor cards: | The ace, king, queen, jack and ten of each suit are called honor cards.

The ten is the only honor card which has no value in terms of high card points. |

Instant Glossary

Opening bid:
(Opener)

The first bid made in any auction, other than pass.

The opener must have at least 13 points to open the bidding.

Response:
(Responder)

When the opener's partner answers him, it's called a response.

The responder needs a minimum of 6 points to respond to the opener.

Book:

The declaring side always has a handicap of six tricks. This handicap is called book.

You add book to the final level reached in the auction to determine how many tricks must be won in the play.

Contract:

The number of tricks which must be won in the play is called your contract.

Instant Glossary

Game:

A designated level of bidding. If your final contract is on a game level, you receive a bonus if you make the required number of tricks.

Major suit and notrump games:

The major suit games are 4♥ and 4♠ and require at least ten tricks in the play. 3NT is the notrump game and needs 9 or more tricks to be successful.

The partnership should hold at least 26 points to contract for game in either notrump or a major suit.

Minor suit games:

The minor suit games are 5♣ and 5♦ and require at least 11 tricks in the play.

Minor suit games should not be bid unless the partnership holds a minimum of 30 points.

Slams:

A slam is a 12 or 13 trick contract which can be bid in any suit or notrump. A small slam (on the sixth level) requires 33 points, while a grand slam (seventh level) needs at least 37.

Finding a fit is only half of bidding. Once you know where the hand should play (notrump or a suit) you must judge how high to bid.

The level you finally stop on dictates how many tricks must be won in the play.

If you bid too high you won't make your contrct. But if you stop too low, your contract may not be worth as much.

Your objective is to bid a game whenever you have a good chance of making it.

This can be as easy as counting your points.

By adding your points to partner's you should know how high to bid.

If you have game, bid it! Otherwise, end the auction as soon as possible.

For example, if you know the partnership lacks enough points for game, you can now acknowledge a fit by passing, instead of raising partner to the next level!

We still suggest possible trump suits, and all rules regarding bidding still apply. But now we can bid point count, too.

This is the second half of bidding.

These contracts pay a game bonus:

$\underline{3NT}$
a 9 trick game.

$\underline{4\heartsuit}$ or $\underline{4\spadesuit}$
10 trick games.

$\underline{5\clubsuit}$ or $\underline{5\diamondsuit}$
11 trick games.

Notrump and major suit games should be bid whenever the partnership holds at least $\underline{26}$ points.

Minor suit games should be bid only if the partnership holds at least $\underline{30}$ points.

With little or no chance for game, end the auction as soon as possible.

Explanation:

An opening bid promises at least 13 points but after that the range can vary widely.

For purposes of giving information, opening bids are divided into two main categories:

A <u>minimum</u> opening bid promises exactly 13 to 15 points.

An <u>intermediate</u> opening bid shows 16 to 18 points.

Opening hands which contain more than 18 points are fairly rare and will be covered separately.

There are three times the opener tells his partner which category his opening bid is:

1. Whenever opener rebids his original suit, he shows point count as well as length.

2. Whenever opener supports his partner's suit, he shows point count as well as a fit.

3. Whenever opener bids notrump, he shows point count as well as having no other available bid.

Here is how this works:

A <u>minimum</u> opening bid contains 13 to 15 points.

     ♠ A J 8 6
     ♡ K Q 10
     ◊ A 4 3
     ♣ 9 8 7

This hand has 14 points and is a minimum opening.

An <u>intermediate</u> opening bid contains 16 to 18 points.

     ♠ A K J 8 4
     ♡ 10 9 6
     ◊ A K Q
     ♣ 10 5

This hand has 17 points and is an intermediate opening bid.

Whenever opener rebids his original suit on the lowest possible level, he shows that his opening bid was a minimum.

West (14)	East (10)
♠ Q 4	♠ A 5 3 2
♡ A Q J	♡ 9 5 4
◇ K Q 5 4 2	◇ A 7 6 3
♣ 9 8 2	♣ Q 10

1.	1D	1.	1S	
2.	2D	2.	P!!	

West rebids his diamonds on the lowest possible level (two level) showing at least 5 diamonds and a minimum opening bid, 13 to 15 points.

East knows that West has at most 15 points. He adds that to his own 10 points and can see that there's no chance for game. Therefore, he confirms the fit by passing, allowing West to play on a lower and safer level.

Notice that the rules concerning suit length still apply. Many bids show suit distribution and point count at the same time.

Whenever opener rebids his original suit by skipping over one level, he shows an intermediate opening bid.

West (16)	East (7)
♠ A J 6	♠ K 5 4 3
♡ K Q J	♡ 6 4 3
◇ J	◇ Q 9 5
♣ K J 9 7 6 4	♣ Q 5 3

1.	1C	1.	1S	
2.	3C	2.	P	

West rebids his clubs by skipping over the second level. This shows an intermediate opening bid (16 to 18 points) as well as a minimum of 5 clubs.

Notes:

East knows that his partner's top point count is 18 and that a total of 30 points is needed for game in a minor.

By adding his own 7 points to his partner's maximum (18) he comes up 5 points short, so he acknowledges the fit by passing.

Remember, always add your points to partner's maximum to determine whether or not you have a chance for game. If he holds instead a minimum, he can pass below game level after you support his suit.

Whenever opener supports his partner's suit by raising it to the lowest possible level, he shows a minimum opening bid.

West (14)	East (7)
♠ K Q 10 8	♠ 9 7 6 3
♡ A J 6 5	♡ K 4
◇ J 4	◇ A 10 8 2
♣ K 8 7	♣ 9 6 5

1.	1C		1.	1D
2.	1H		2.	1S
3.	2S		3.	P

West supports spades by raising them to the lowest possible level. This shows a minimum opening bid (13 to 15 points) as well as a fit.

East adds his 7 points to his partner's maximum (15) and passes because there's no chance for game. If East held at least 12 points, he would bid 4♠ instead of passing because the partnership totals enough points to provide a good play for game.

Whenever your partner makes a bid that indicates point count, you will know his total within 2 or 3 points.

If you have a game, you must bid it! So...

Add your points to partner's maximum to prove there's no chance for game,

or add your points to his minimum to prove there is!

If you have game, bid it! Otherwise, end the auction as soon as possible.

Whenever opener supports his partner's suit by skipping over one level, he shows an intermediate opening bid.

West (17)	East (6)
♠ Q 6 4 2	♠ A 9 7 5 3
♡ A 10 7	♡ Q 5 4
♢ A K Q 2	♢ 7 6
♣ Q 2	♣ 9 5 3
1. 1D	1. 1S
2. 3S	2. P

When West supports spades by jumping to the three level (he skipped over the two level) he promises an intermediate opening bid (16 to 18 points) as well as a fit.

Once again, East adds his points (6) to his partner's maximum (18) and passes when he sees they are short of game.

A quick review:

Opener shows a minimum opening bid (13 to 15 points) by:

    1. rebidding his original suit on the lowest possible level.

    2. supporting his partner's suit by raising it to the lowest possible level.

Opener shows an intermediate opening bid (16 to 18 points) by:

    1. rebidding his original suit and skipping over one level.

    2. supporting his partner's suit and skipping over one level.

Bid these hands!

1.

West: (13)

♠ K Q 10 9 6 4
♡ A 2
◇ J 2
♣ K 4 3

Note: when
opener rebids
his original
suit on the
lowest level,
it shows a
minimum opening.

1. _____	1. _____
2. _____	2. _____
3. _____	3. _____
4. _____	4. _____
5. _____	5. _____
6. _____	6. _____

East: (9)

♠ J 3
♡ K 9 8 5 3
◇ Q 10 9
♣ Q J 10

Note: when you know
there's no chance for
game, end the auction
as soon as possible.

2.

West: (14)

♠ K J 5 4
♡ Q J 9 8 6
◇ K Q
♣ Q 10

Note: when
opener has a
fit and 13 to
15 points, he
raises
responder's
suit one level.

1. _____	1. _____
2. _____	2. _____
3. _____	3. _____
4. _____	4. _____
5. _____	5. _____
6. _____	6. _____

East: (8)

♠ 10 8 7 3
♡ A 2
◇ 8 6 4 3
♣ A 9 6

3.

West: (16)

♠ A J
♡ K Q J 8
◇ A J 10 4 3
♣ 7 3

Note: when
opener has a
fit and 16 to
18 points, he
raises
responder's
suit two levels.

1. _____	1. _____
2. _____	2. _____
3. _____	3. _____
4. _____	4. _____
5. _____	5. _____
6. _____	6. _____

East: (11)

♠ K 3 2
♡ A 10 9 3 2
◇ K 8
♣ J 5 4

Note: when you've
found your fit, if
you know you have
a game, bid it!

Answers:

1. West   East

   1. 1S (46)   1. 1NT (33)
   2. 2S (46 & 79)   2. P (77)

East responds 1NT because he cannot bid a new suit (hearts)
on the two level without at least 10 points. West rebids
his spades by raising them to the lowest possible level.
This promises at least 6 spades and a minimum opening bid.
East confirms the fit by passing because he knows there is
no chance for game.

2. West   East

   1. 1H (46)   1. 1S (27)
   2. 2S (28 & 80)   2. P (77)

West acknowledges the fit in spades by raising the suit
one level. This shows a minimum opening bid as well as a
fit. East adds his 8 points to the maximum number his
partner can hold (15) and knows that there is no chance
for game, so he passes.

3. West   East

   1. 1D (47)   1. 1H (27)
   2. 3H (28 & 81)   2. 4H (77)
   3. P   3. ____

West supports his partner's hearts by raising the suit
two levels. By skipping over a level, he promises an
intermediate opening bid. This time East adds his 11
points to his partner's minimum (16 points) and knows
that game will be a comfortable proposition.

Add your points to partner's maximum to prove there is
no chance for game, or add your points to his minimum,
to prove there is.

Note: Remember to go back and review the explanations
       if you missed any of the bids.

Explanation:

Responses can also vary in point count. You must have at least 6 points to respond, but it's possible to hold considerably more.

Responses are divided into two categories:

A <u>minimum</u> response guarantees 6 to 11 points.

An <u>intermediate</u> response shows 12 to 15 points.

Responding hands which hold more than 15 points will be discussed separately.

Responder will announce his point count on three different occasions:

1. Whenever responder rebids his original suit, he shows point count as well as length.

2. Whenever responder supports his partner's suit, he shows point count as well as a fit.

3. Whenever responder bids notrump, he shows point count as well as having no other available bid.

Responder gives point count in exactly the same situations as the opener. Only the amount of points are different.

After partner has opened:

A <u>minimum</u> response contains 6 to 11 points.

♠ K J 6 4 3
♡ Q 7 6
♢ J 9 4
♣ 10 7

This hand has 7 points and is a minimum response.

An <u>intermediate</u> response contains 12 to 15 points.

♠ 8 5
♡ A K J 6
♢ K Q 10
♣ 9 7 5 4

This hand has 13 points and is an intermediate response.

Whenever responder rebids his original suit on the lowest possible level, he shows a minimum response.

West (14)   East (7)

♠ K J 6 5   ♠ 10 9 4
♡ Q 4   ♡ K J 10 9 8
♢ Q 3   ♢ K 5 4
♣ A Q 9 8 7   ♣ 6 2

1. __1C__   1. __1H__
2. __1S__   2. __2H__
3. __P!!__   3. _____

West bids 1♠ at his second turn to show a new suit on the one level before rebidding his first suit (clubs) on a higher level. East rebids hearts on the lowest possible level. This promises 5 or more hearts and a minimum (6 to 11 points) response.

West adds his 14 points to his partner's maximum (11) and knows that game is very improbable. He passes, even though they might not have a fit. Remember, East has promised only 5 hearts. The safety factor of playing at a lower level more than compensates for the incomplete fit.

You can allow partner to play at a lower level, without a fit, when game is unlikely.

Whenever responder rebids his original suit by skipping over a level, he shows an intermediate response.

West (15)   East (13)

♠ K Q   ♠ J 8 6
♡ A 10 9   ♡ K Q J 8 7 4
♢ J 8   ♢ K Q 10
♣ K Q 5 4 3 2   ♣ J

Notes:

1.	1C	1.	1H
2.	2C	2.	3H
3.	4H	3.	P

When East rebid his hearts he skipped over the second level. This shows an intermediate response, 12 to 15 points, and a minimum of 5 hearts.

West adds his 15 points to partner's minimum (12) and knows that game is odds on, so he bids it.

Whenever the partnership holds a minimum opening and an intermediate response, bid a game!

Whenever responder supports his partner's suit by raising it to the lowest possible level, he shows a minimum response.

West (14)	East (7)
♠ A J 9 7 4	♠ K Q 10
♡ K Q 4 2	♡ J 8
◇ A 10 8	◇ 7 6 3 2
♣ 3	♣ J 8 5 4

1.	1S	1.	2S
2.	P	2.	

When East raises spades to the lowest possible level, he shows a minimum (6 to 11 points) as well as a fit. West passes, because even if East has maximum point count (11 points) it's not enough for game.

Whenever responder supports his partner's suit by skipping over one level, he shows an intermediate response.

Notes:

West (13)	East (12)
♠ A J 6	♠ K 4 3
♡ Q 9 8	♡ K 10
◊ Q J 10 7	◊ A 9 5 3 2
♣ K 9 4	♣ Q 10 6

	West		East
1.	1D	1.	3D
2.	3NT!!	2.	P

When East supports diamonds by jumping to the third level (he skipped over the second level) he promises an intermediate response (12 to 15 points) as well as a fit.

There are two points of interest regarding West's final bid of 3NT.

First, in spite of a fit in diamonds, West knows the partnership lacks enough points for game in a minor. However, they definitely are in the game zone for notrump. West bids the game because East can always bid 4◊ if he feels his hand is very unsuitable for notrump play.

Second, you can see that both West and East have an absolute minimum point count for their bids. This gives the partnership only 25 points, 1 below the game requirement.

Once in a while this will happen and you will have to play your contract as well as you can. The bonus for making your game will more than offset the times you don't.

When you have a minimum opening bid opposite an intermediate response, game must always be bid somewhere! If you cannot play in a minor suit fit, try notrump. If your fit is in a major, bid game there. This rule applies to the responder (when his suit has been supported) as well as to the opener.

A quick review:

Responder shows a minimum response (6 to 11 points) by:
1. rebidding his original suit on the lowest possible level.

2. supporting his partner's suit by raising it to the lowest possible level.

Responder shows an intermediate response (12 to 15 points) by:
1. rebidding his original suit and skipping over one level.

2. supporting his partner's suit and skipping over one level.

Allow partner to play at a lower and safer level (even with no fit) when you know there is no chance for game.

When one partner has a minimum opening and the other has an intermediate response, game should always be bid somewhere!

If you have too few points for game in your minor suit fit, try 3NT.

Bid these hands:

1.

West: (14)

♠ A 5 4
♡ 6 5
♢ K Q 10 9 4
♣ A J 10

Note: a minimum opening opposite an intermediate response always produces game somewhere.

East: (13)

♠ Q J 9
♡ A K J 10 9
♢ 3 2
♣ Q 4 3

Note: when responder rebids his original suit and skips a level, it shows an intermediate response.

West		East	
1.	_____	1.	_____
2.	_____	2.	_____
3.	_____	3.	_____
4.	_____	4.	_____
5.	_____	5.	_____
6.	_____	6.	_____

2.

West: (7)

♠ 10 9 8
♡ A Q 9
♢ 8 6 4 3 2
♣ J 9

Note: when responder has a fit and 6 to 11 points, he raises opener's suit one level.

East: (14)

♠ A Q J 6
♡ K J 10 4
♢ Q J 10
♣ 5 3

West		East	
1.	_____	1.	_____
2.	_____	2.	_____
3.	_____	3.	_____
4.	_____	4.	_____
5.	_____	5.	_____
6.	_____	6.	_____

3.

West: (13)

♠ K J 10 8
♡ A K
♢ J 10 9 8
♣ J 4 3

Note: when you know you have a game, bid it!

East: (13)

♠ Q 5 4 3
♡ J 9 5 3
♢ A Q 3
♣ A 9

Note: when responder has a fit and 12 to 15 points, he raises opener's suit two levels.

West		East	
1.	_____	1.	_____
2.	_____	2.	_____
3.	_____	3.	_____
4.	_____	4.	_____
5.	_____	5.	_____
6.	_____	6.	_____

Answers:

1. West   East

    1.   1D (47)   1.   1H (27)
    2.   2D (47 & 79)   2.   3H (30 & 85)
    3.   3NT (33 & 77)   3.   P

This is a tough one. West rebids his diamonds at the
lowest possible level, showing a minimum opening bid and
5 or more diamonds. East rebids his own suit, hearts,
and skips over the second level. This shows 5 or more
hearts and an intermediate response.

West knows that they have enough points for game, but
he doesn't have a fit in hearts. He tries 3NT and this
is acceptable to East who ends the auction by passing.

Remember, a minimum opening bid opposite an intermediate
response is always enough points to contract for game.
If you don't have a fit, try notrump!

2. West   East

    1.   P   (44)   1.   1D (47)
    2.   2D (47 & 86)   2.   P

West doesn't have enough points to open, so he passes.
When West supports East's diamonds by raising them to
the lowest possible level, he shows a minimum response
(6 to 11 points) as well as a fit. East passes because
he knows there's no chance for game.

3. West   East

    1.   1D (47)   1.   1H (27)
    2.   1S (27)   2.   3S (28 & 85, 86)
    3.   4S (77 & 86)   3.   P

When East supports his partner's spades by skipping
over the two level, he shows an intermediate response
as well as a fit. West knows they have a game so he
bids it.

Whenever you know you have a game, bid it!

COMING UP:

More about Showing Point Count

Invitations to Bid Game

Recommended time: 45 to 55 minutes

Explanation:

Whenever opener or responder bids notrump, it's because he has no other available bid. For that reason, a notrump bid always gives point count.

Whenever the opener rebids notrump, he describes his hand in terms of minimum and maximum.

A minimum notrump rebid by the opener shows 13 to 15 points and no other available bid.

A maximum notrump rebid by the opener shows at least 20 points and no other available bid.

The intermediate opening bid, 16 to 18 points, is never used for a notrump rebid. Whenever opener holds an intermediate opening which is suitable for play in notrump, he opens the bidding with 1NT.

This unorthodox opening will be covered in a section entitled "special opening bids" which appears shortly after this chapter.

Whenever opener rebids notrump at the lowest possible level, he shows a minimum opening bid.

West (14)	East (8)
♠ A J 9	♠ K 8 6 4
♡ 10 5 4	♡ J 9 8 3
◇ K Q 9 5	◇ A 2
♣ K J 5	♣ 8 6 4

1.	1D	1.	1H
2.	1NT	2.	P

When West rebids 1NT he shows a minimum opening bid (13 to 15 points) as well as no other available bid. East does not mention spades, because West would have

Important:

When the opening bidder has exactly 19 points and wishes to rebid in notrump, he bids 2NT.

He skips over the 1 level and bids notrump on the 2 level.

This is called an invitation to game and will be discussed later.

rebid 1♠ (instead of 1NT) if he had 4 spades. As the partnership does not have enough points for game, East passes 1NT, allowing West to play on a low level.

Whenever opener rebids game in notrump, he shows a maximum opening bid.

West (20)   East (9)

♠ K 8 4   ♠ A Q 3 2
♡ K Q J 6   ♡ 4 3 2
♢ A 10   ♢ K 8 5 4
♣ A Q J 3   ♣ 8 5

1. __1C__   1. __1D__
2. __1H__   2. __1S__
3. __3NT__   3. __P__

West runs out of bids, so he jumps all the way to game (third level) in notrump. This shows a maximum opening (at least 20 points) and no other available bid.

When you reach the section on high level bidding (slams and grand slams), big hands, such as the one above, may be bid in a different, more exploratory manner.

But for now, whenever the opener has no available bid and enough points to try for game opposite a minimum response, he should rebid 3NT.

When you know you have a game, bid it; otherwise partner may pass below game level and eliminate all bonus possibilities.

Notes:

Explanation:

The responder bids notrump with no other bid available. He continues to show point count in terms of minimum and intermediate.

A <u>minimum</u> notrump response shows 6 to 11 points.

An <u>intermediate</u> notrump response shows 12 to 15 points.

Whenever responder bids notrump on the lowest possible level, he shows a minimum response.

<u>West</u> (13)	<u>East</u> (8)
♠ K Q 8	♠ J 7
♡ J 4 3 2	♡ Q 10 8
◇ A K 9 2	◇ J 5 4
♣ 4 2	♣ A 9 8 7 3

1.	1D	1.	1NT
2.	P	2.	____

After West opens, East would like to bid his clubs. But if responder's first bid is a new suit on the two level, he shows 10 or more points and at least 5 cards in his suit. East bids 1NT, showing a minimum response (6 to 11 points) and no other bid. West passes because there is no chance for game.

Whenever responder bids notrump by skipping over one level, he shows an intermediate response.

<u>West</u> (14)	<u>East</u> (12)
♠ 8 5 4 3	♠ A Q J
♡ K J	♡ 10 9 8 7
◇ A Q 10	◇ J 9 5
♣ K J 8 5	♣ A 10 3

Notes:

```
1.   1C        1.   1H
2.   1S        2.   2NT
3.   3NT       3.   ____
```

East responds 1♡ and West rebids
1♠. Notice that their points are
not in those suits. When East
rebids notrump, he has skipped
over the second level. This shows
an intermediate response (12 to
15 points) as well as nothing
else to bid. West knows they have
enough points for game, so he bids
it.

A quick review:

Whenever opener or responder
bids notrump, it always
shows point count!

Opener shows a minimum
opening (13 to 15 points) by
rebidding notrump at the
lowest possible level.

Opener shows a maximum
opening (20 or more points)
by rebidding game in notrump.

Responder shows a minimum
response (6 to 11 points)
by bidding notrump at the
lowest possible level.

Responder shows an inter-
mediate response (12 to 15
points) by bidding notrump
and skipping over one
level.

Both opener and responder
bid notrump only with no
other available bid.

Bid these hands:

1.

West: (13)

♠ A K J 10 9 8
♡ 7
◇ K J 6
♣ J 4 3

East: (7)

♠ 4
♡ K Q 8 5 4 2
◇ Q 3 2
♣ 10 6 2

Note: when responder bids notrump at the lowest possible level, he shows a minimum response.

1. _____	1. _____
2. _____	2. _____
3. _____	3. _____
4. _____	4. _____
5. _____	5. _____
6. _____	6. _____

2.

West: (8)

♠ K Q 10
♡ J 8 4
◇ Q 8 3
♣ 10 8 7 5

Note: when responder bids notrump at the lowest possible level, he shows a minimum response.

East: (21)

♠ A 8 7
♡ A Q 5 2
◇ A J 9 5
♣ A Q

Note: when opener rebids game in notrump he shows a maximum opening bid.

1. _____	1. _____
2. _____	2. _____
3. _____	3. _____
4. _____	4. _____
5. _____	5. _____
6. _____	6. _____

3.

West: (14)

♠ K Q
♡ A 10 9 8
◇ Q 7 4
♣ K 6 4 3

Note: when opener rebids notrump at the lowest possible level, he shows a minimum response.

East: (13)

♠ A 10 5 3
♡ K 5
◇ A J 9 5
♣ J 10 8

Note: when you know you have a game, you must bid it!

1. _____	1. _____
2. _____	2. _____
3. _____	3. _____
4. _____	4. _____
5. _____	5. _____
6. _____	6. _____

Answers:

1.   West   East

      1.   __1S__ (46)   1.   __1NT__ (33 & 93)

      2.   __2S__ (46 & 79)   2.   __P__

East responds by bidding notrump on the lowest possible
level. This shows a minimum response as well as no
other bid. West rebids his spades on the lowest level,
showing 6 or more spades and a minimum opening bid.

East passes even without a fit, because the partnership
doesn't have enough points for game. West, with at least
6 spades, should be relatively safe at the two level.

2.   West   East

      1.   __P__   (44)   1.   __1D__ (47)

      2.   __1NT__ (33 & 93)   2.   __3NT__ (92)

      3.   __P__   3.   ____

West passes because he doesn't have enough points to
open. After West responds 1NT, showing a minimum response,
East bids game in notrump. This shows a maximum opening
bid. Notice that East doesn't suggest hearts, because if
West held 4 hearts, he would have bid them in preference
to 1NT.

3.   West   East

      1.   __1C__ (47)   1.   __1D__ (27)

      2.   __1H__ (27)   2.   __1S__ (27)

      3.   __1NT__ (33 & 91)   3.   __3NT__ (77)

      4.   __P__   4.   ____

When West bids 1NT he shows a minimum opening bid. East
knows the partnership has enough points for game, so he
bids 3NT. When you know you have game, bid it!

Notice that neither partner showed point count until
West bid 1NT. In general, you are not allowed to pass
until someone shows point count. If you pass without
knowing your partner's count, you may miss a game.

Explanation:

Even after the opener or responder gives point count, there are times when more information will be required to bid a game.

For example, you hold this 16 point hand and open 1♠:

    ♠ A K J 8 5 2
    ♡ K Q 6
    ◊ 5 4
    ♣ K 10

Partner responds 2♠, showing a minimum response, 6 to 11 points.

But which is it? Does he hold 6 points or closer to 11?

If he holds the minimum, you have no chance for game. But if he has 10 or 11 points, game would be a good proposition.

How can you find out?

Whenever you want a clearer range of your partner's point count, bid one more of the agreed suit.

With the hand presented above, you would now bid 3♠. This is still one level below game and invites your partner to bid the game if he has the top of his previous bid.

What you are saying is,"Partner, you have supported spades and that is where we will play the hand. But I need more information to determine if we have a game. If you are at the top of your 2♠ bid (10 or 11 points) bid the game, otherwise pass."

If partner has a bad hand and passes, you should make 3♠ more often than not.

Here are some more examples:

West (13)　　　East (11)

♠ K 8 5 4　　♠ A 9 3 2
♡ Q J 3　　　♡ A 8 2
♢ A Q　　　　♢ J 4
♣ J 7 6 4　　♣ Q 8 3 2

1.　1C　　　1.　1S
2.　2S　　　2.　3S
3.　P　　　　3.　_____

East does not support clubs
because West might have opened a
3 card suit. When West shows a
minimum opening bid by raising
spades one level, East knows that
game is possible. If West has the
top of his bid (15 points) game
should be bid, otherwise not.

East invites West to game by
raising the agreed suit one level.
West, on a dead minimum, passes.

Notice that the responder as well
as the opener can invite to game.

West (17)　　　East (10)

♠ A K J　　　♠ 6 5 3
♡ A K Q 3 2　♡ 8 6
♢ 4 3 2　　　♢ A Q 10 5
♣ 6 4　　　　♣ K J 9 5

1.　1H　　　1.　1NT
2.　2NT　　　2.　3NT
3.　P　　　　3.　_____

East can't bid a new suit on the
two level for his first response
because he doesn't have a 5 card
suit. He bids 1NT, showing a
minimum response. West knows that
if East is at the top of his
response, they have a game. He
invites him by bidding 2NT and
East is happy to accept.

Notice that you can invite in
notrump as well as a suit.

Important:

When the opener holds exactly
19 points and wishes to rebid
in notrump, he invites to
game by bidding 2NT.

West (19)　　　East (9)

♠ A J 7　　　♠ 10 8 4
♡ K 5　　　　♡ A Q 8 4
♢ K Q J 6　　♢ 8 7 5
♣ A J 3 2　　♣ K 10 9

1.　1C　　　1.　1H
2.　2NT　　　2.　3NT
3.　P　　　　3.　_____

West opens 1♣ and East
responds 1♡. Now West has no
available bid so he shows
point count by rebidding 2NT.
This also invites East to bid
game in notrump with at least
7 points.

East bids the game and West
passes.

You have now completed the final
phase of basic bridge play, and
should spend the next few hours
practicing all you have learned.

Ideally, you should play with
other beginners but this is not
always possible.

If you enter a game with more
experienced players, ask them to
be patient because you still have
much to learn.

You don't know, for example, the
rules for entering the auction
after one of the opponents has
opened the bidding. Nor should
you try to absorb them. If you
hold a big hand and an opponent
opens, you will have to pass.

And there are many difficult hands
which present a choice of bids
and there are some bidding rules
you don't know yet.

Don't even think about slams.
If you're dealt a great number of
points just bid to game. That
should be your main objective--bid
those games!

If you don't know what to bid in
a particular situation, do the
best you can. Make the bid which
comes closest to the rules you
know.

Don't worry about play technique
or what card to lead, just play!
If you're the declarer get used to
playing from the right hand (yours
or dummy's).

Above all, don't let anyone teach
you new material. This will only
confuse you because you need a
solid foundation before moving on.

This book will cover everything you
need to become an adequate bridge
player and experience will do the
rest.

Notes:

Questions:

1. What contract is game in notrump?

2. What contracts are the major suit games?

3. What contracts are the minor suit games?

4. How many points does the partnership need for game in notrump?

5. In a major suit?

6. In a minor suit?

7. What is the exact point range of a minimum opening bid?

8. How about an intermediate opening bid?

9. What is the exact point range of a minimum response?

10. An intermediate response?

11. When are the three times you show point count, either as opener or responder?

12. What do you do if you need more information from your partner to determine whether or not you have a game?

Answers:

1. 3NT.

2. 4♡ and 4♠.

3. 5♣ and 5◊.

4. at least 26 points.

5. at least 26 points.

6. at least 30 points.

7. 13 to 15 points.

8. 16 to 18 points.

9. 6 to 11 points.

10. 12 to 15 points.

11. whenever you rebid your original suit, support your partner's suit or bid notrump.

12. invite your partner by raising the agreed suit (or notrump) to the next highest level below game.

Optional Review:

1.

West: (14)

♠ A 2
♥ K Q J 4 3 2
♦ K J 5
♣ 3 2

East: (7)

♠ J 10 9 6
♥ A 8 7
♦ 8 3 2
♣ Q 9 6

1. ____	1. ____
2. ____	2. ____
3. ____	3. ____
4. ____	4. ____
5. ____	5. ____
6. ____	6. ____

2.

West: (14)

♠ 6 4 3
♥ A J 5 3
♦ A Q J
♣ Q 5 4

East: (7)

♠ A Q J 5 2
♥ 10 8
♦ 8 5 4
♣ 9 8 7

1. ____	1. ____
2. ____	2. ____
3. ____	3. ____
4. ____	4. ____
5. ____	5. ____
6. ____	6. ____

3.

West: (13)

♠ K Q
♥ A K 3 2
♦ 10 9 8
♣ J 8 7 6

East: (14)

♠ J 2
♥ J 6 5 4
♦ A K J 3 2
♣ A 2

1. ____	1. ____
2. ____	2. ____
3. ____	3. ____
4. ____	4. ____
5. ____	5. ____
6. ____	6. ____

Answers:

1. West   East

    1. 1H (46)   1. 2H (46 & 86)
    2. P   2. ____

When East supports his partner's hearts, he shows a
minimum response. West passes, knowing that there's
no game.

2. West   East

    1. 1D (51)   1. 1S (27)
    2. 1NT (33 & 90)   2. 2S (30 & 85)
    3. P   3. ____

With two 3 card minors, West opens the one with better
high cards. When West bids 1NT he shows a minimum
opening bid as well as nothing else to say. East rebids
spades, showing at least 5 and a minimum response. West
passes because there's no chance for game.

3. West   East

    1. 1C (47)   1. 1D (27)
    2. 1H (27)   2. 3H (28 & 85, 86)
    3. 4H (77)   3. P

When East supports his partner's hearts by skipping over
one level, he shows an intermediate response. West bids
the game because a minimum opening bid opposite an
intermediate response should usually produce enough
points for game.

Optional Review:

4.

West: (14)

♠ A Q 5 3
♡ 9 5 4
♢ K Q J 3 2
♣ Q

East: (9)

♠ J 4 2
♡ K 6 3 2
♢ A 8 7
♣ J 9 8

1. _____   1. _____
2. _____   2. _____
3. _____   3. _____
4. _____   4. _____
5. _____   5. _____
6. _____   6. _____

5.

West: (14)

♠ A 9 4
♡ Q
♢ A K 10 9 5
♣ J 10 9 8

East: (14)

♠ K 8 6 5
♡ K J 5 4
♢ Q J
♣ A 4 2

1. _____   1. _____
2. _____   2. _____
3. _____   3. _____
4. _____   4. _____
5. _____   5. _____
6. _____   6. _____

6.

West: (16)

♠ J 5
♡ A Q 9 8 6 4
♢ K Q J
♣ K 3

East: (8)

♠ K Q 6
♡ 5 3 2
♢ 10 4
♣ Q J 8 7 4

1. _____   1. _____
2. _____   2. _____
3. _____   3. _____
4. _____   4. _____
5. _____   5. _____
6. _____   6. _____

4.   West   East

1.   _1D_ (47)   1.   _1H_ (27)
2.   _1S_ (30)   2.   _1NT_ (33 & 93)
3.   _2D_ (47 & 79)   3.   _P_

East bids 1NT showing a minimum response and West rebids his diamonds (after bidding a new suit on the one level) showing a minimum opening. East passes because there's no game.

5.   West   East

1.   _1D_ (27 & 47)   1.   _1H_ (27)
2.   _2C_ (33)   2.   _3NT_ (33 & 77, 93)
3.   _P_   3.   ____

West opens 1◊ because he is bidding his longest minor. He can rebid 2♣ because clubs ranks below diamonds. This bid shows at least 4 clubs and, therefore, at least 5 diamonds. East is not interested in a minor suit game so he bids 3NT.

6.   West   East

1.   _1H_ (46)   1.   _2H_ (46 & 86)
2.   _3H_ (97)   2.   _P_ (97)

East supports hearts at the lowest level, showing a minimum response. West needs more information to determine whether or not they have a game. He invites his partner to game by bidding one more of the agreed suit. This asks East if he has the top of his 2♡ bid (10 or 11 points) to bid the game. With a bad hand, East refuses the invitation by passing.

Now that you know how to play
bridge, you should be practicing
with other players.

You should continue your play
sessions, even as you are working
your way through the last half of
this book.

None of the following chapters
have time limits, so just play
them at your own pace.

Don't try to memorize
anything.

I recommend that you
finish one chapter per
evening, but proceed at
your own rate.

You should finish each
chapter almost as fast as
it would take for a
normal reading.

COMING UP:

Special Play Techniques

Leading toward Your High Cards

Communication

The Finesse

The following section will explain
three special play techniques. If
you played your way through the
optional hands in the preceding
sections, you are already halfway
home.

In the hand diagrams which
illustrate the explanations, the
compass position of each player is
not usually given.

North is always the hand
positioned nearest to the top of
the page and South is closest to
the bottom.

West is to the far left and East
is to the far right.

Occasionally, abbreviations will
denote compass location. N.
stands for North, S. for South,
and so on.

The play problems which follow
each technique section will
continue to be presented with most
of the cards having already been
played.

South will be the declarer and
North the dummy. West and East
will be the defenders.

Notes:

Leading
toward your
high cards:

The basic principle
of all bridge play!

In order to take full
advantage of your high
cards, you should always
attempt to lead up to them.

Whenever you or the dummy
has a high card in a suit
you wish to lead, the first
card should be led from the
opposite hand.

In the diagram, South is
the declarer and the only
suit shown is spades. South
would like to win a trick with
dummy's king, but to achieve
this, he must make the initial
lead from the South hand.

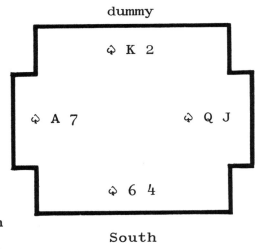

dummy

♠ K 2

♠ A 7   ♠ Q J

♠ 6 4

South

He leads the ♠4 and West is in a quandary. If he plays the
ace, dummy's king will win the second trick, but if he
follows low, the king will win immediately.

No player can win a trick in progress if he has already
played a losing card. If West does play low, he cannot
take his card back when South plays dummy's king.

East may have the ♠A, but in that case, dummy's king will
never win a trick. Remember, East plays after the dummy,
so the ace would capture the king.

Notice that if the first card is led from the dummy, South
will lose two tricks no matter where the ace is.

```
        N
W               E
        S
```

Leading toward your
high cards:

South would like to win
a trick with the ◊J. To
do so, the first card
must be led from the
opposite hand.

Assume North has the lead.
South plays dummy's ◊2 and
no matter which card East
decides to play, the ◊J
will win a trick, either
now or later.

dummy

◊ 4 2

◊ 9 8   ◊ K 5

◊ J 6

South

The one time you do not
have to lead up to your
high card is when that
card is already a winner.

In the diagram, dummy's
♡A will always win one
trick whether you lead
up to it or not.

dummy

♡ A 2

♡ J 9   ♡ Q 7

♡ 6 5

South

Play these hands!

South is the declarer on all play problems.

1. There is no trump suit.

    South leads the ♣5 and West follows with the ♣3. What card should South play from dummy?

    Why?

1.

    North
    ♠ ---
    ♡ ---
    ♢ ---
    ♣ K 4

    West   East
    ♠ ---   ♠ ---
    ♡ ---   ♡ ---
    ♢ ---   ♢ ---
    ♣ A 3   ♣ J 9

                South
                ♠ ---
                ♡ ---
                ♢ ---
                ♣ 6 5

2. There is no trump suit.

    What is the high card you would like to win a trick with?

    Which hand must lead the first card in order for you to have a chance to win a trick?

2.

    North
    ♠ ---
    ♡ 6 4
    ♢ ---
    ♣ ---

    West   East
    ♠ ---   ♠ ---
    ♡ 5 3   ♡ 10 8
    ♢ ---   ♢ ---
    ♣ ---   ♣ ---

                South
                ♠ ---
                ♡ 9 2
                ♢ ---
                ♣ ---

Analysis:

1.

North
- ♠ ---
- ♡ ---
- ◇ ---
- ♣ K 4

West
- ♠ ---
- ♡ ---
- ◇ ---
- ♣ A 3

East
- ♠ ---
- ♡ ---
- ◇ ---
- ♣ J 9

South
- ♠ ---
- ♡ ---
- ◇ ---
- ♣ 6 5

There <u>is</u> <u>no</u> <u>trump</u> <u>suit</u>!

South should try to win the trick with dummy's king.

If West has the ♣A (you can see he does) then the ♣K will win this trick.

If East has the ace, then dummy's king will not win a trick because East plays after the dummy.

When you lead toward a high card, you have a 50% chance to win a trick with it.

If you do not lead toward your high cards, you will rarely win a trick with them.

2.

North
- ♠ ---
- ♡ 6 4
- ◇ ---
- ♣ ---

West
- ♠ ---
- ♡ 5 3
- ◇ ---
- ♣ ---

East
- ♠ ---
- ♡ 10 8
- ◇ ---
- ♣ ---

South
- ♠ ---
- ♡ 9 2
- ◇ ---
- ♣ ---

There <u>is</u> <u>no</u> <u>trump</u> <u>suit</u>!

South would like to win a trick with his ♡9. Notice that a "high" card does not have to be an honor.

Sometimes late in the play, even a 5 or a 6 may have a chance to win a trick if you lead up to it.

South must lead the first card from the dummy (North) to take advantage of his ♡9.

```
┌─────────────────────────┐
│                         │
│  Communication:         │
│                         │
│                         │
└─────────────────────────┘
```

The art of transportation;
crossing over from one hand
to the other.

There are times when you'd
like to lead up to a high
card but your are
uncomfortably placed in the
wrong hand to do so.

You must then find a way
to "cross over" to the
opposite hand before you
can complete your
objective.

dummy

♦ A
♣ 6 4

♦ J   ♦ 9
♣ 5 2   ♣ K 9

♦ 6
♣ Q 3

South

In the diagram, South is the
declarer and also has the
lead. He wants to lead up
to his ♣Q, but he is in the
wrong hand. He must find some way to get over to the
dummy so he can lead up to his high card.

This means he must enter dummy in another suit before he
can correctly play the club suit. Therefore, South plays
the ♦6 and dummy wins with the ace.

Now South is in the hand opposite his high card and can
lead toward it.

The ♦A is called an entry because it allows declarer
access to the opposite hand.

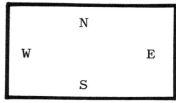

Communication.
Transportation.
Entry.

An entry is not always
a high card winner.

Diamonds are trump and
South has the lead. He
would like to get to the
dummy to lead toward his
♡Q.

He leads the ♠8 and trumps
it in dummy with the ◊8.
Now he is in the right hand
to lead up to his high card.

This time his entry was a
trump.

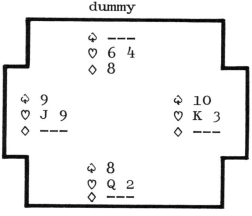

dummy

```
              ♠ ---
              ♡ 6 4
              ◊ 8
♠ 9                        ♠ 10
♡ J 9                      ♡ K 3
◊ ---                      ◊ ---
              ♠ 8
              ♡ Q 2
              ◊ ---
```

South

Your entry does not have to
be an immediate winner.

South is on lead and there
is no trump suit. He leads
the ♠4 toward dummy's king.
Assume West wins the trick
by playing the ace and,
after dummy and East follow
low, West leads the ♠8.

This time dummy's king will
win, enabling South to lead
up to his own high card, the
♡Q.

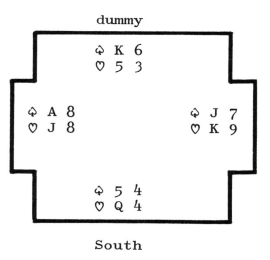

dummy

```
              ♠ K 6
              ♡ 5 3
♠ A 8                      ♠ J 7
♡ J 8                      ♡ K 9
              ♠ 5 4
              ♡ Q 4
```

South

Play these hands!

South is the declarer.

1. There is no trump suit.

   What is the high card South would like to lead up to?

   Which hand does he want to lead the first card from?

   Assume that South is on lead. How can he cross over to the dummy?

2. Spades are trump.

   South is on lead and wants to win all 3 tricks.

   How is this possible?

1.

North
♠ ---
♡ J
♢ 3 2
♣ ---

West
♠ ---
♡ 10 7
♢ 4
♣ ---

East
♠ ---
♡ ---
♢ K J 9
♣ ---

South
♠ ---
♡ 4
♢ Q 8
♣ ---

2.

North
♠ 2
♡ A K
♢ ---
♣ ---

West
♠ ---
♡ 9
♢ J 4
♣ ---

East
♠ ---
♡ ---
♢ A Q
♣ J

South
♠ ---
♡ ---
♢ 8 6
♣ 10

Analysis:

1.

North
- ♠ ---
- ♡ J
- ◇ 3 2
- ♣ ---

West
- ♠ ---
- ♡ 10 7
- ◇ 4
- ♣ ---

East
- ♠ ---
- ♡ ---
- ◇ K J 9
- ♣ ---

South
- ♠ ---
- ♡ 4
- ◇ Q 8
- ♣ ---

<u>There <u>is</u> <u>no</u> trump suit</u>!

South would like to lead up to his ◇Q, but first, he must cross over to the dummy.

South leads the ♡4 to dummy's jack in order to play a diamond toward his queen.

2.

North
- ♠ 2
- ♡ A K
- ◇ ---
- ♣ ---

West
- ♠ ---
- ♡ 9
- ◇ J 4
- ♣ ---

East
- ♠ ---
- ♡ ---
- ◇ A Q
- ♣ J

South
- ♠ ---
- ♡ ---
- ◇ 8 6
- ♣ 10

<u>Spades</u> <u>are</u> <u>trump</u>!

This time South has no high cards to lead up to.

But he wants to get to dummy for a different reason. The ace and king of hearts are winners, if only South can cross over to cash them.

If South leads either a diamond or a club, he can trump it in dummy and then score his heart winners, taking all 3 tricks.

Notice that communication serves other purposes besides leading toward your high cards!

```
┌─────────────────────┐
│                     │
│   The finesse:      │
│                     │
│                     │
└─────────────────────┘
```

An attempt to win an extra
trick by rendering one of
the opponent's high cards
worthless.

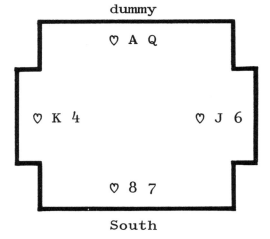

There are times when it seems
that you must lose a trick,
when actually that is not the
case at all.

The art of making an
opponent's "sure" winner
disappear is called a
finesse.

In the diagram, South is
on lead and wants to win 2
tricks. He leads the ♡7
and West follows low. If he
now makes the "normal" play
of winning with dummy's ace, he will lose the next trick
to West's king. Instead, he should play dummy's queen.

East plays after dummy and can't win the trick since he
doesn't have the king. West, who does have the king,
has already followed with a losing card and has no
chance to win the trick.

West's sure winner has vanished.

If East had the king, South would lose one trick, which he
would have lost anyway by refusing the finesse and playing
dummy's ace. In other words, South breaks even when the
finesse loses.

But when it succeeds, which it will 50% of the time, South
wins an extra trick.

```
┌─────────────────────┐
│          N          │
│  W               E  │
│          S          │
└─────────────────────┘
```

You can devalue an opponent's
high card by trapping it
between your hand and dummy's.
This is also called a finesse.

South leads the ◊Q and West
follows low. If South
plays dummy's ace, he will
lose the next trick to the
king. Instead, he plays
dummy's 2, and because
East does not have the king,
South's queen will win the
trick.

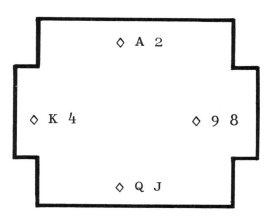

Notice that West's honor
card is trapped. If he
covers the queen, the ace
will capture his king,
promoting South's jack into
a winner.

Often, you must combine
techniques to play your
cards to best advantage.

South would like to win an
extra trick with the ♣J, but
in order to take a finesse,
he must first cross over to
the dummy.

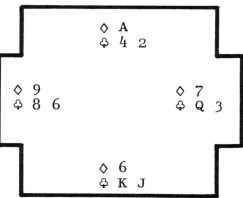

So before playing clubs, he
uses dummy's ◊A for transportation. Now he takes the
finesse, which as you can see, wins.

Notice that if he led the first club from his hand, he
would lose the jack, no matter which opponent held the queen.

Play these hands!

South is the declarer.

1. There is no trump suit.

    South leads the ♡2 and West follows low. What card should South play from dummy?

    Why?

2. Spades are trump.

    South is on lead and wants to win all 4 tricks. What card should South play first?

    Why does South want to cross over to the dummy?

    How can South win all 4 tricks?

1.

North
♠ ---
♡ A K J
♢ ---
♣ ---

West   East
♠ ---   ♠ ---
♡ Q 8 4   ♡ 9 7 6
♢ ---   ♢ ---
♣ ---   ♣ ---

South
♠ ---
♡ 5 3 2
♢ ---
♣ ---

2.

North
♠ K
♡ ---
♢ Q J 10
♣ ---

West   East
♠ J   ♠ ---
♡ 3 2   ♡ 6
♢ 5   ♢ K 8 6
♣ ---   ♣ ---

South
♠ 2
♡ ---
♢ A 7 4
♣ ---

Analysis:

1.

North
♠ ---
♡ A K J
◊ ---
♣ ---

West
♠ ---
♡ Q 8 4
◊ ---
♣ ---

East
♠ ---
♡ 9 7 6
◊ ---
♣ ---

South
♠ ---
♡ 5 3 2
◊ ---
♣ ---

There _is_ _no_ _trump_ _suit_!

South leads the ♡2 and West follows low. South should insert dummy's jack. He hopes that West has the ♡Q and by taking the finesse, he can render it worthless.

2.

North
♠ K
♡ ---
◊ Q J 10
♣ ---

West
♠ J
♡ 3 2
◊ 5
♣ ---

East
♠ ---
♡ 6
◊ K 8 6
♣ ---

South
♠ 2
♡ ---
◊ A 7 4
♣ ---

Spades _are_ trump!

If South wants to win all 4 tricks, he had better lead the ♠2 to dummy's king!

South plays a spade for two reasons. First, he wnats to extract the outstanding trump because he doesn't want an opponent trumping one of his winners. And second, he wants to cross over to the dummy and take the diamond finesse.

If he plays as described, he'll win all 4 tricks. After reaching the dummy, South will lead the ◊Q and trap East's king. If East plays low, the queen will win and if he covers, the ace will capture his king. This promotes dummy's jack and ten into winners.

The finesse is important enough to present two extra play problems. South is still the declarer.

3.   There is no trump suit.

South is on lead and wants to win all 3 tricks.

Obviously, he hopes that West has the ◇K and can be finessed out of it.

What should be the first card South leads?

3.

North
♠ ---
♡ ---
◇ A J 10
♣ ---

West
♠ ---
♡ ---
◇ K 5 4
♣ ---

East
♠ ---
♡ ---
◇ 9 8 6
♣ ---

South
♠ ---
♡ ---
◇ Q 3 2
♣ ---

4.   Spades are trump.

South is on lead and must win all 4 tricks.

Assume South leads the ♣2 and West follows with the ♣6. What card should South play from dummy?

Dummy wins the first trick. What card should South lead off the dummy to start the second trick?

4.

North
♠ 2
♡ ---
◇ ---
♣ A Q 10

West
♠ 6
♡ ---
◇ ---
♣ K J 6

East
♠ 8
♡ ---
◇ ---
♣ 7 5 4

South
♠ A
♡ ---
◇ ---
♣ 9 8 2

Analysis:

3.

North
♠ ---
♡ ---
◊ A J 10
♣ ---

West
♠ ---
♡ ---
◊ K 5 4
♣ ---

East
♠ ---
♡ ---
◊ 9 8 6
♣ ---

South
♠ ---
♡ ---
◊ Q 3 2
♣ ---

There <u>is</u> <u>no</u> <u>trump</u> <u>suit</u>!

South should lead the ◊Q. If West holds the ◊K (he does) South can win all 3 tricks by taking the finesse.

But look what happens if South starts out by leading a small diamond. West plays low and South plays dummy's jack (or ten) which wins the trick. The lead is now in the dummy.

South can cash the ◊A, but must lose the third trick to West's king.

If South originally leads the ◊Q, the finesse still wins when West follows low. The difference is that South remains in hand to repeat the finesse.

4.

North
♠ 2
♡ ---
◊ ---
♣ A Q 10

West
♠ 6
♡ ---
◊ ---
♣ K J 6

East
♠ 8
♡ ---
◊ ---
♣ 7 5 4

South
♠ A
♡ ---
◊ ---
♣ 9 8 2

<u>Spades</u> <u>are</u> <u>trump</u>!

If South wants to win all of the tricks, he must play dummy's ♣10 This is called a double finesse. South hopes that West has both missing club honors (he does) and can be finessed out of them.

After dummy's ♣10 wins the first trick, South must re-enter his hand to take another finesse. He does this by leading dummy's ♣2 to his ace. Notice that even though the opponents have outstanding trump, South cannot afford to draw them right away. The trump ace is his only entry back to his hand.

Questions:

1. What is the basic principle of all bridge play?

2. When is the one time you don't have to lead up to a high card?

3. Crossing over from one hand to the other is called...?

4. What is an entry?

5. Does an entry have to be an immediate winner?

6. What is a finesse?

7. Is a finesse a sure thing?

8. What percentage of the time should you expect your finesses to win?

9. What is a double finesse?

Answers:

1. leading toward your high cards.

2. when your high card is already a winner.

3. communication or transportation.

4. a winning card which allows access to the opposite hand.

5. no, an opponent may win a trick (or tricks) before one of your cards is promoted into a winning entry.

6. an attempt to win an extra trick by rendering an opponent's high card worthless.

7. no.

8. 50%.

9. an attempt to win 2 extra tricks by rendering worthless two high cards, held by the same opponent.

Bid these hands: Optional Review

1.

West: (20)   East: (8)

♠ A Q J 5   ♠ 8 7 4
♡ A J 6 4   ♡ K 3 2
♢ K Q 10   ♢ A 4 3
♣ K 10   ♣ J 8 5 4

1. _____   1. _____
2. _____   2. _____
3. _____   3. _____
4. _____   4. _____
5. _____   5. _____
6. _____   6. _____

2.

West: (14)   East: (12)

♠ J   ♠ K Q
♡ K Q 5 4   ♡ J 10 9 6 3
♢ A 5 4 2   ♢ K Q J
♣ K J 7 6   ♣ 10 9 3

1. _____   1. _____
2. _____   2. _____
3. _____   3. _____
4. _____   4. _____
5. _____   5. _____
6. _____   6. _____

3.

West: (17)   East: (10)

♠ A K 10 8 7   ♠ Q 6 5
♡ A Q J   ♡ 8 4
♢ 6 5   ♢ K Q 4 3
♣ K 8 5   ♣ Q J 3 2

1. _____   1. _____
2. _____   2. _____
3. _____   3. _____
4. _____   4. _____
5. _____   5. _____
6. _____   6. _____

Answers:

1. West   East

    1. __1D__ (51)   1. __1NT__ (33 & 93)
    2. __3NT__ (77)   2. __P__

East responds 1NT, showing a minimum response and no other available bid. West has enough points to bid a game in notrump, so he bids it.

2. West   East

    1. __1C__ (47)   1. __1H__ (27)
    2. __2H__ (28 & 80) 2. __4H__ (77)
    3. __P__   3. ____

When West supports his partner's hearts, he shows a minimum opening bid as well as a fit. East knows the partnership had enough points for game in a major, so he bids it.

3. West   East

    1. __1S__ (46)   1. __2S__ (46 & 86)
    2. __3S__ (97)   2. __4S__ (97)
    3. __P__   3. ____

When East supports spades, he shows a minimum response and a fit. West needs more information to determine whether or not the partnership has a game, so he invites East by bidding 3♠. This requests East to bid the game if he has the top of his 2♠ response, 10 or 11 points. With 10 points, East obliges by bidding the game.

COMING UP:

Special Opening Bids

Notrump Openings

Strong Two Bids

Pre-empts

There are some instances when the opening bid will describe the opener's hand within highly defined limits. The opener not only shows suit distribution, but also provides his approximate point count or trick-taking potential.

These special bids are called:

Notrump openings
Strong Two Bids
Pre-empts

As you read through this section, it's more important to remember the purpose of these bids rather than to try to memorize the rules which define them.

Explanation:

The opener may wish to suggest right from the opening bid that the hand be played in notrump.

He can open notrump on any of the first 3 levels; each bid shows a different point count:

A 1NT opening promises 16 to 18 points.

2NT shows 22 to 24 points.

3NT announces 25 to 27 points.

If you are going to play without any trump, you should have a lot of high cards because you cannot trump anything.

Besides point count, there are other factors which make your hand suitable for notrump play.

Whenever you open notrump, you make a statement regarding your suit distribution. You promise partner that your hand is divided almost evenly (balanced) among the four suits.

Your hand must not contain any voids or singletons (see enclosed column) and you are allowed at most 1 doubleton.

Short suits such as voids or singletons are much more valuable in a suit contract where you can trump some of the opponents' winners than in notrump where you cannot.

Finally, you cannot open notrump unless you have a stopper or protected honor card in at least 3 suits. Remember, when you are the declarer, the opponent to your left will make the opening lead.

New terms:

Void: When you sort your hand and find no cards in any given suit (---) you are said to be void in that suit.

Singleton: Only 1 card in any given suit.

Doubleton: Only 2 cards in any given suit.

Tripleton: 3 cards in any given suit.

Stopper: A protected honor card.

If he leads a long suit headed by the top honors, he could cash enough tricks to break your contract before you even obtained the lead. Look at this hand:

♠ 4 3 2
♡ A K Q 10
♢ A K Q 10
♣ 3 2

You are the declarer and have 18 points, more than enough to open the bidding. You also have an even or balanced distribution. But if you are thinking about notrump, forget it!

What happens if you declare a notrump contract and partner also has little strength in spades and clubs?

In spite of all your points the opponents could win every single trick!

And as they were running their black suit winners you would end up discarding all those lovely aces and kings.

When you play in notrump, high card wins. If you can't follow suit you have no chance to win the trick.

So before you open notrump, make sure that you're protected in at least 3 suits. You would like stoppers in all of the suits, but "perfect" notrump hands are rarely dealt. And because notrump openings give partner more information than any other bid, it's worth a slight risk to make them more frequently.

The accepted stoppers are given in the enclosed column.

Remember, a notrump opening defines your hand within exact limits. Make sure that you meet every requirement.

Accepted Stoppers:

An <u>ace</u> is a stopper all by itself.*

A <u>king</u> needs to be supported by a lower card to be a stopper.

A <u>queen</u> must be accompanied by 2 lower cards.

A <u>jack</u> must have 3-card support to be a stopper.

If you have two or more honor cards in the same suit, only the highest honor needs to be protected.

*Even so, you can't open notrump with a singleton ace, because you're not allowed to have a singleton!

Here is a quick review:

Whenever you open the bidding by suggesting notrump, you show:

A specific number of points. 1NT is 16 to 18, 2NT promises 22 to 24 and 3NT is 25 to 27.

Balanced or even suit distribution. No voids, no singletons and at most 1 doubleton.

A stopper or protected honor card in at least 3 suits.

You must meet all three stipulations before you can open the bidding in notrump. And if you meet these requirements you <u>must</u> open in notrump!

Notes:

Whenever the opener opens 1NT he shows 16 to 18 points, even distribution and stoppers in at least 3 suits.

West (18)   East (8)

♠ K Q   ♠ A 8 5
♡ 9 7 2   ♡ K 10 8
◊ A Q 5 4 3   ◊ J 8 2
♣ A Q J   ♣ 7 5 3 2

1. 1NT   1. 2NT
2. 3NT   2. P

West opens 1NT rather than 1◊, because he gives his partner a greater amount of information about his hand. In general, always open in notrump if you are able to do so, even with a 5 card suit.

East cannot bid the game because he doesn't know if the partnership holds enough points. Game in notrump requires at least 26 points. If West holds 16 or 17, they probably can't make it. But if he has 18, they probably can.

East invites his partner to game by responding 2NT. This asks West to bid 3NT with a full 18, and he does.

After partner opens 1NT, the rules for the responder are very simple. Either the partnership has enough points to bid a game or not.

If responder holds under 8 points, he passes. Game has little chance even if opener has 18.

If responder has exactly 8 or 9 points, he invites by bidding 2NT. Partner will bid game with 18.

If responder holds 10 or more points, he bids 3NT. The partnership has at least 26 points even if opener has only 16.

Notes:

Whenever the opener opens 2NT he shows 22 to 24 points, even distribution and a stopper in at least 3 suits.

Responder should bid game (3NT) with 4 or more points, otherwise he should pass.

West (23)   East (5)

♠ K Q J   ♠ A 3 2
♡ A Q 5   ♡ J 6 4
♢ A Q 8 2   ♢ 6 4 3
♣ K Q 2   ♣ 8 7 4 3

1. __2NT__   1. __3NT__
2. __P__   2. _____

After West opens 2NT, East knows that the partnership holds enough points for game so he bids it. If East held under 4 points he would have passed.

Whenever the opener opens 3NT he shows 25 to 27 points, balanced distribution and stoppers in at least 3 suits.

Responder passes because 3NT is game.

West (27)   East (0)

♠ A K J   ♠ 6 4 3 2
♡ A K J   ♡ 7 5 4
♢ K Q 10 9 8   ♢ 6 3
♣ A Q   ♣ 9 8 7 6

1. __3NT__   1. __P__

West opens the bidding by contracting for game in notrump and East passes. East has what is often referred to as a Yarborough, a hand with absolutely no honor cards. Even so, West has a good chance to win 9 tricks.

Notes:

A word to responders:

Whenever partner opens in notrump you know his exact point range. Your sole obligation is to bid a game if you think the partnership has at least 26 points and to pass if you don't.

The only time you can invite is when partner opens 1NT and you have exactly 8 or 9 points.

Once in a while partner will open in notrump and you'll hold a big hand. Even if you know you have considerably more than 26 points, just bid to game.

Notrump slams will be discussed later, in "high level bidding."

A quick review:

Whenever opener opens in notrump he shows an exact point count range.

    1NT shows 16 to 18.
    2NT shows 22 to 24.
    3NT shows 25 to 27.

Opener also shows even distribution. No voids, no singletons and at most 1 doubleton.

Finally, opener promises a stopper (protected honor card) in at least 3 suits.

Bid these hands:

1.

West: (12)

♠ A Q 8
♡ K 8 5
◊ K 7 6 2
♣ 7 6 3

Note: if partner opens 1NT, bid game with 10 or more points.

East: (17)

♠ K J 10
♡ A 4 3 2
◊ Q J 8
♣ K Q J

	West		East
1.	_____	1.	_____
2.	_____	2.	_____
3.	_____	3.	_____
4.	_____	4.	_____
5.	_____	5.	_____
6.	_____	6.	_____

2.

West: (16)

♠ 8 7 6
♡ A K J 4
◊ K Q J 2
♣ Q 3

Note: in order to open 1NT, your hand must meet all requirements!

East: (11)

♠ K Q 4
♡ Q 8 7 5 3
◊ A 3
♣ 8 6 4

	West		East
1.	_____	1.	_____
2.	_____	2.	_____
3.	_____	3.	_____
4.	_____	4.	_____
5.	_____	5.	_____
6.	_____	6.	_____

3.

West: (18)

♠ A J
♡ K J 7
◊ A J 10 5 4
♣ A 3 2

East: (8)

♠ K Q 9
♡ 10 8 5 3
◊ Q 2
♣ J 7 6 5

Note: if partner opens 1NT, invite to game with 8 or 9 points.

	West		East
1.	_____	1.	_____
2.	_____	2.	_____
3.	_____	3.	_____
4.	_____	4.	_____
5.	_____	5.	_____
6.	_____	6.	_____

Answers:

1. West   East

    1. P   (44)   1. 1NT (130)
    2. 3NT (130)   2. P

West lacks enough points to open so he passes. East
opens 1NT showing 16 to 18 points, even distribution
and a stopper in at least 3 suits. West knows they have
enough points for game in notrump, so he bids it.

2. West   East

    1. 1D   (47)   1. 1H (27)
    2. 3H   (28 & 81)   2. 4H (77)
    3. P   3. ____

Even though West has 16 to 18 points and even distribution,
he can't open 1NT because he doesn't have 2 suits stopped.
He has no protection in the black suits so he opens 1◊.
After his partner responds 1♡, West shows an intermediate
opening bid by supporting hearts and skipping over one
level. East knows the partnership has game so he bids
it.

3. West   East

    1. 1NT (130)   1. 2NT (130)
    2. 3NT (130)   2. P

West meets all requirements and opens 1NT. With 8 points,
East doesn't know whether or not the partnership has a
game so he invites West by bidding 2NT. With the top of
his notrump opening (18 points) West accepts by bidding
the game. If he had fewer points he would refuse the
invitation by passing.

Explanation:

Occasionally, you'll pick up such a strong hand that you should have a reasonable play for game even if partner has no high cards.

If your hand has even distribution, 25 to 27 points and stoppers, you can open by bidding game in notrump. But what if your hand has uneven distribution? What if you would rather play in a suit contract?

Obviously, if you make the normal opening bid of 1 in your long suit, partner will pass with under 6 points and a potential game will vanish.

You prevent this from happening by opening your suit on the two level.

An opening bid of 2♣, 2♢, 2♡ or 2♠ cannot be passed even if partner has zero points! This is called a strong two opening and both partners must continue bidding until a game (or slam) has been reached.

If you are going to force partner to keep bidding, knowing that his hand may be worthless, you must be sure that your own hand can produce enough tricks for game or very close to it.

Before you even consider opening a strong two bid, your hand should meet these requirements:

You must have a solid suit or a very long semi-solid suit. If you have two long suits, they must both be semi-solid or better.

You must have at least 4 quick tricks, divided among two or three suits.

New terms:

<u>Solid</u> <u>suit</u>: A long suit which usually plays for no losers.

<u>Semi-solid</u> <u>suit</u>: A long suit which usually plays for no more than two losers.

<u>Quick</u> <u>tricks</u>: Honor cards or a combination of honor cards which almost always win tricks, whether you are declaring or defending.

Let's look at each in turn.

A long suit is one which has at least 5 cards. In order for your suit to be considered solid, it should usually play for no losers.

For example, these suits would be considered solid:

1. ♠ A K Q J 9
2. ♠ A K Q 10 9 5
3. ♠ A K J 10 9 8 5 3

If you play these suits by first cashing the top honors, you would not normally expect to lose any spade tricks.

The longer your suit is, the fewer top honors it needs to be regarded as solid.

A semi-solid suit is one which usually plays for no more than 2 losers. Again, your suit must be at least 5 cards in length.

These suits are semi-solid:

1. ♠ A Q 10 9 5
2. ♠ K J 10 9 8
3. ♠ Q J 10 9 5 4

Even if partner offered you little support, you would normally expect to lose at most 2 spade tricks in the play.

A quick trick is an honor card or a combination of honor cards which almost always wins a trick or tricks, whether your side is declaring or defending.

For example, aces almost always win a trick (unless they are trumped) as opposed to queens and jacks which are far from sure winners.

Here is a list of acceptable quick tricks. These are the only honor cards or combinations which can be counted.

When you hold an ace and king in the same suit, count 2 quick tricks.

When you hold an ace and queen in the same suit, count 1 1/2 quick tricks.

When you hold an ace or a king and queen in the same suit, count 1 quick trick.

When you hold a king protected by at least one lower card other than the queen, count 1/2 quick trick.

Whenever opener starts the bidding at 2 of a suit, he promises a good suit or suits which can play with little or no support from partner and at least 4 quick tricks.

West (21)

♠ A Q
♡ A K Q 10 9 6
◇ 7 5 3
♣ A Q

East (4)

♠ K J 6 5 3
♡ 3
◇ 10 8 4 2
♣ 9 7 6

1.	2H	1.	2NT!!
2.	3H	2.	3S
3.	4H	3.	P

West has 5 quick tricks and a solid suit so he opens 2♡. East has only 4 points but can't pass until the partnership has reached a game.

Notice that East's first response is 2NT. Whenever responder has only 1 quick trick or less, he makes the bid of 2NT to inform partner that he has a bad hand. This is called a negative response and gives West a clear message.

"Partner, we must bid to game because you opened a strong two bid. But if you are thinking about a slam, expect no help from me. I have a bad hand!"

After East gives the negative response of 2NT, he's free to bid his spade suit. But West wants to play in hearts and bids the game.

Notice that West did not rebid 4♡ after his opening bid. The partnership has been committed to bid a game. This allows West to move slowly in order to learn more about his partner's hand.

After partner opens a strong two bid, responder gives a negative response with 1 quick trick or less, even with a fit!

West (21)	East (1)
♠ A Q J 9 6	♠ 10 8 7 5
♡ A K J 9 8	♡ 7 5
♢ A Q	♢ 8 6 4 2
♣ 7	♣ J 8 6

	West		East
1.	2S	1.	2NT
2.	3H	2.	3S
3.	4S	3.	P

This time West has 2 semi-solid suits and 5 quick tricks so he opens 2♠. With 2 five-card suits he still opens the higher one first. East has a good fit but no quick tricks. Therefore, he must make the negative response of 2NT before he shows his fit.

West now bids his second suit (hearts) and East supports spades. West bids the game and should have a very good chance to make it, in spite of the fact that the partnership has fewer points than are normally required to contract for game.

A strong two opening is based more on playing tricks than on counting points between the two hands. Even though West and East total only 22 points, 10 tricks should present little difficulty.

Experience is a good teacher and the more you play, the better you will be able to estimate the trick-taking potential of any given hand.

After partner opens a strong two bid, responder gives a positive response with more than 1 quick trick.

West (22)
♠ K Q J
♡ A Q J 7 6 5
♢ K Q
♣ A 2

East (7)
♠ A 8 7 5
♡ 10 8 2
♢ 7 4 3 2
♣ K 8

West		East	
1.	2H	1.	3H
2.	4H	2.	P

West has a good semi-solid suit and 4 1/2 quick tricks so he opens 2♡. East has 1 1/2 quick tricks, enough for a positive response, so he shows his fit immediately by raising hearts. Usually, a strong two bid opposite a positive response indicates good slam potential. For now, just bid to game. Slam bidding will be discussed later.

In the above hand, if East didn't have a fit in hearts he could have suggested another suit if it was at least 5 cards in length.

Notes:

Whenever responder bids a new suit (as his first response) over a strong two opening, he promises more than 1 quick trick and at least 5 cards in his suit.

After partner opens a strong two bid, responder bids 3NT with more than 1 quick trick, no fit with opener (3-card support) and without a 5 card (or longer) suit.

West (21)   East (9)

♠ A K J   ♠ 8 5 4 2
♡ Q   ♡ K 6 3
◇ A 4 2   ◇ K 9 7 5
♣ A Q J 10 4 3   ♣ K 6

1. __2C__   1. __3NT__
2. __4C__   2. __5C__
3. __P__   3. ____

West has a good semi-solid club suit and 4 1/2 quick tricks, so he opens 2♣. East has 1 1/2 quick tricks and must give a positive response. But he has no fit and no 5-card suit to bid. He announces a positive response and no other available bid by bidding 3NT.

West would play in notrump if his hand was suitable, but it isn't. He has only a singleton heart and is afraid of losing too many heart tricks to score a notrump game. He repeats clubs, showing at least 6-card length and East now has a fit and bids the game.

A quick review:

Opener can commit the partnership to game by opening in a suit on the two level.

He must have at least 4 quick tricks and a solid suit; or a long semi-solid suit; or two long suits which are semi-solid or better.

Responder shows a negative response (1 quick trick or less) by bidding 2NT.

He shows a positive response (more than 1 quick trick) by:

Raising his partner's suit;

Bidding a new suit of at least 5 cards in length;

Bidding 3NT with no other available bid.

Bid these hands: 1.

West: (9)   East: (22)

♠ K Q 8 3   ♠ A J
♡ A   ♡ K Q J 10 5 2
◊ 10 8 5 4   1. _____   1. _____   ◊ A K
♣ 9 8 5 3   ♣ K J 2

Note: after   2. _____   2. _____   How many quick
partner opens   tricks are in this
a strong two   3. _____   3. _____   hand?
bid, with a
positive re-   4. _____   4. _____
sponse and no
available bid,   5. _____   5. _____
bid 3NT.
                 6. _____   6. _____

                                          2.

West: (23)   East: (5)

♠ K Q J   ♠ 10 4
♡ A Q J 10   ♡ 7 3 2
◊ K J 4   ◊ Q 9 5 3
♣ A Q 3   1. _____   1. _____   ♣ K 8 7 5

                 2. _____   2. _____

                 3. _____   3. _____

                 4. _____   4. _____

                 5. _____   5. _____

                 6. _____   6. _____

                                          3.

West: (23)   East: (1)

♠ A K Q   ♠ J 9 8 7 6 4
♡ A K Q 9 7 5   ♡ 6
◊ 8   ◊ 10 7 5
♣ K Q 10   1. _____   1. _____   ♣ 9 6 4

How many   2. _____   2. _____   Note: after partner
quick tricks   opens a strong two
are in this   3. _____   3. _____   bid, with a negative
hand?   response bid 2NT. You
                 4. _____   4. _____   can always show your
                                                 suit or a fit later.
                 5. _____   5. _____

                 6. _____   6. _____

Answers:

1. **West**   **East**

   1. <u>P</u> (44)   1. <u>2H</u> (137)
   2. <u>3NT</u> (140)   2. <u>P</u>

West cannot open the bidding because he doesn't have
13 points. East has a semi-solid suit and 4 1/2
quick tricks so he opens 2♡.

West has 2 quick tricks, more than enough for a
positive response, but he has no available bid. He
doesn't have a fit and he has no 5-card (or longer)
suit so he bids 3NT which relays this information to
East.

This time East's hand is suitable for play in notrump
so he passes.

2. **West**   **East**

   1. <u>2NT</u> (131)   1. <u>3NT</u> (131)
   2. <u>P</u>   2. <u>   </u>

With 22 to 24 points, even distribution and at least
3 suits stopped, West opens 2NT. East bids the game
because he has 4 or more points.

3. **West**   **East**

   1. <u>2H</u> (137)   1. <u>2NT</u> (138)
   2. <u>3H</u> (46)   2. <u>3S</u> (138)
   3. <u>4S</u> (28, 77)   3. <u>P</u>

West has a solid suit and 5 quick tricks so he opens
2♡. East has no quick tricks so he responds 2NT. This
warns his partner to proceed with caution. West rebids
his hearts and now East introduces his spade suit.
West has a fit in spades so he bids 4♠ and East passes.

Explanation:

As soon as you play through several deals of bridge, you'll find that you're dealt many more bad hands than good ones.

Most of the time you must resign yourself to passing or hoping that partner can bid, allowing you to respond with a suitable hand.

But once in a while your bad hand will contain a long suit, either broken or semi-solid. If you also hold no more than 1/2 quick tricks outside of your suit, you can open the bidding with a pre-empt.

A pre-empt or shut-out bid is an opening bid on the three or four level and is mainly defensive in nature.

The pre-empter hopes that if the opponents have strong hands, they will find it difficult to enter the bidding once the auction has started out on a high level.

A pre-empt always shows a bad hand with one long playable suit.

The pre-empter does not normally expect to make his contract but hopes for one of two things to happen:

If the opponents decide to defend, he may fall several tricks short of making his bid, but will profit anyway if the opposition could have made a game or even a slam.

New terms:

Pre-empt or
Shut-out bid: An obstructive bid, made on a high level, which makes it difficult for the opponents to enter the auction.

Broken suit: A long suit which normally plays for more than 2 losers.

Playable suit: Usually a long suit, always headed by at least the queen and jack.

Sacrifice: Deliberately bidding to a contract you do not expect to make, in order to prevent the opponents from making their own contract.

Ruff or Ruffing: Means the same thing as to trump or trumping. Whenever you cannot follow suit you can win the trick by trumping or "ruffing" it.

This is called a sacrifice. The pre-empter is willing to pay a small penalty for going down in his contract if he can prevent the opponents from receiving a game or slam bonus.

And even if the opponents decide to enter the auction, they are forced to do so on a high and uncomfortable level.

This gives them a good chance of bidding too high or choosing to play in the wrong contract.

A word of caution to prospective pre-empters: Don't pre-empt indiscriminately! If partner has a strong hand you cause him the same problems you hoped to give the opponents.

What's worse, if partner has a smattering of high cards, you may go down in your contract when the opponents have no chance of making anything.

You can pre-empt whenever you are the dealer or when neither of the opponents has opened in front of you.

Later, after you've learned about competitive bidding, you will be allowed to pre-empt even after one of the opponents has opened the bidding.

In order to pre-empt, you must have a broken or semi-solid suit of at least 7 cards in length. Because you are starting out on the third or fourth level, your suit should have some high card protection.

Notes:

In general, you shouldn't consider pre-empting unless your suit is headed by at least the queen and jack. This is regarded as a playable suit.

Whenever you have a playable 7-card suit and little outside honor strength, open the bidding on the three level.

West (7)   East (14)

♠ J 5 4   ♠ A Q 3
♡ ---   ♡ K Q 8 6 4 2
◊ Q J 9 8 7 5 3   ◊ 10
♣ K 5 3   ♣ Q J 2

1. _3D_   1. _P_

West, with a bad hand and a long playable diamond suit with only 1/2 quick trick outside, opens 3◊.

East's pass provides several points of interest.

First, he passes even though he has the point count for an opening bid. His partner has told him (by pre-empting) that he has a bad hand, with little or no chance for game.

Second, East passes even though he has a 6-card heart suit. West may have no hearts at all, and if East becomes the declarer in a heart contract, the dummy may give him zero tricks.

Third, East passes because he hopes the opponents will enter the auction. He has good chances to beat their final contract. Who knows, they may even end up in hearts.

Notes:

Whenever you have a playable suit which contains 8 cards (or longer) and little outside honor strength, open the bidding on the four level.

West (6)	East (14)
♠ 7 5	♠ A Q 3
♡ 3	♡ K Q 8 6 4 2
◇ A Q 9 7 6 4 3 2	◇ 10
♣ 9 8	♣ Q J 2

| 1. | 4D | 1. | P |

West, with a bad hand and a playable 8-card diamond suit, opens 4◇. East has the same hand as in the previous example and passes for exactly the same reasons.

Whenever partner opens on the three level, you need 4 1/2 quick tricks to raise to game in a major and at least 5 1/2 for game in a minor.

If partner opens on the four level in a minor, you need 4 1/2 quick tricks to raise to game.

West (6)	East (18)
♠ K Q J 8 7 6 3	♠ 10 4
♡ 9 7	♡ A K 8 6
◇ 3	◇ A Q 4 2
♣ 10 4 2	♣ A J 6

| 1. | 3S | 1. | 4S |
| 2. | P | 2. | ___ |

West meets the requirements for a shut-out bid and opens 3♠. With 4 1/2 quick tricks, East raises him to game. Technically, they don't have the points for game, but the long suit and quick tricks more than compensate.

Do not pre-empt when you have more than 1/2 quick tricks outside of your suit or when

Notes:

your suit is not playable.

<u>West</u> (8)   <u>East</u> (14)

♠ 10 8 7 6 4 3 2   ♠ 9 5
♡ A 4 2   ♡ K Q 7 6
◊ A 3   ◊ K 10
♣ 7   ♣ K Q J 10 8

1. <u>P</u>   1. <u>1C</u>
2. <u>1S</u>   2. <u>2C</u>
3. <u>2S</u>   3. <u>P</u>

Even though West has a 7-card
suit, it's not considered a
playable suit. Even if his suit
were better, he still couldn't
pre-empt because he has too many
quick tricks outside of his suit.
So he passes and awaits developments.

East opens 1♣ and West responds
1♠. Both rebid their suits
showing a minimum for their first
bid. East passes 2♠, letting his
partner play on a low and
relatively safe level.

It may seem ill advised to play
in a trump suit which is missing
almost all of the top honors,
but unless one opponents has all
4 missing cards, at least two
of the honrs will fall together
when you play the spade suit.

There's only one time you can
pre-empt after partner has
opened the bidding.

After partner has opened 1 in a
major suit, you can raise to
game with a bad hand and at least
5-card trump support.

You must also hold 1 outside
quick trick and some ruffing
value, either a singleton or a
void. This is another way of
shutting out the opponents.

Notes:

West (13)

♠ K J 9 8 6
♡ A 6 3
◊ J 8 7
♣ A 5

East (6)

♠ Q 10 4 3 2
♡ 7
◊ A 10 9
♣ 9 8 7 4

1. __1S__   1. __4S__
2. __P__   2. _____

After West opens 1♠, East with
5-card support, 1 outside quick
trick and some trumping value
(singleton heart) pre-empts all
the way to game. This bid serves
a dual purpose.

Even though the partnership
technically lacks the point count
to try for game, the super trump
fit and good ruffing value make
4♠ a better than average
proposition.

And if the worst happens and the
game goes down, the opponents
reap only a small reward. But
they were effectively shut out
from finding their heart fit
where they might have a game.

Notice that the opponents have
9 hearts between them, but in
order for either of them to bid
they must start on the five
level!

The pre-empt by responder after
partner opens a major is an
extremely potent weapon and can
be used to great advantage.

You no longer need the 6 points
which are required to respond,
when you raise partner's major
to game. But you must meet all
of the rules necessary to make
this shut-out bid. Otherwise,
pass or respond normally.

A quick review:

You can pre-empt whenever
you are dealer or if no one
has opened in front of you.

With a playable 7-card suit
open on the three level.
With a playable 8-card
suit open on the four level.

Do not pre-empt when your
hand contains more than 1/2
quick trick outside of
your suit.

Responder can pre-empt when
partner opens a major if he
has a bad hand, 5-card (or
more) trump support, an
outside quick trick and
some ruffing value.

Bid these hands: 1.

West: (8)   East: (13)

♠ A J 9 8 7 6 4 3   ♠ Q
♡ K 7   ♡ Q J 9 6 4
♢ 6 5   ♢ A Q J
♣ 4   ♣ J 9 8 5
                  1. _____   1. _____
                  2. _____   2. _____
                  3. _____   3. _____
                  4. _____   4. _____
                  5. _____   5. _____
                  6. _____   6. _____

                                    2.

West: (4)   East: (14)

♠ A 5 4   ♠ K 2
♡ 10 9 6 4 3 2   ♡ A J 8 7 5
♢ 8   ♢ 10 7 6 4
♣ 8 5 4   1. _____   1. _____   ♣ A Q

Note: when   2. _____   2. _____
partner opens   3. _____   3. _____
a major,
raise to game   4. _____   4. _____
with 5-card   5. _____   5. _____
(or more)   6. _____   6. _____
support, an
outside quick trick,
trumping value and a bad hand!

                                    3.

West: (6)   East: (20)

♠ 6 5   ♠ A K 9 8 7
♡ 8 5   ♡ A Q 10 7
♢ K Q J 7 6 4 3   ♢ ---
♣ 9 4   ♣ A K 8 7

                  1. _____   1. _____   Note: when partner
                  2. _____   2. _____   opens a minor on the
                                             three level, raise
                  3. _____   3. _____   to game with 5 1/2
                  4. _____   4. _____   or more quick
                                             tricks.
                  5. _____   5. _____
                  6. _____   6. _____

Answers:

1. **West**   **East**

    1.   <u>4S</u> (146)   1.   <u>P</u>

West opens 4♠ because he has a playable 8-card suit, only
1/2 quick trick outside of his suit, and a bad hand. East
passes because 4♠ is game.

2. **West**   **East**

    1.   <u>P</u>   (44)   1.   <u>1H</u> (46)
    2.   <u>4H</u> (147, 148)   2.   <u>P</u>

West certainly doesn't have enough points to open and
under normal circumstances he wouldn't even have enough
to respond. But after his partner opens 1♥, his hand
meets every requirement to pre-empt to game. He shut-outs
the opponents by bidding 4♥ and East passes.

3. **West**   **East**

    1.   <u>3D</u> (145)   1.   <u>5D</u> (146)
    2.   <u>P</u>   2.   <u>   </u>

West opens 3◊. This promises a playable 7-card suit,
no more than 1/2 quick trick outside of his suit and
a bad hand. East has 5 1/2 quick tricks and raises
his partner to game.

It may seem risky to raise your partner on a void, but
he has already told you that that's the only suit he
wishes to play in. In fact, 5◊ is the only game which
has a good chance of making.

Play these hands!

South is the declarer for all four play problems.

1. Hearts are trump.

South is on lead and wants to win all 4 tricks. What card should South lead first?

Why?

Whenever you decide South should cross over to dummy, which card should be the first one led from dummy?

Why?

2. There is no trump suit.

South is on lead and must win all 4 tricks. He leads the ♠4 and West follows low. What card should South play from dummy and why?

When South is ready to play the heart suit, which hand (South or North) should lead the first card?

Assume South plays the ♡10 off dummy and East follows low. What card should South play and why?

1.

North
♠ ---
♡ A
♢ Q J 5
♣ ---

West
♠ ---
♡ K
♢ 7 6 4
♣ ---

East
♠ ---
♡ 10
♢ K 3 2
♣ ---

South
♠ ---
♡ J
♢ A 10 9
♣ ---

2.

North
♠ A Q
♡ 10 9
♢ ---
♣ ---

West
♠ K 7
♡ 4 2
♢ ---
♣ ---

East
♠ J 5
♡ Q 8
♢ ---
♣ ---

South
♠ 8 4
♡ K J
♢ ---
♣ ---

Analysis:

1.

North

♠ ---
♡ A
♢ Q J 5
♣ ---

West

♠ ---
♡ K
♢ 7 6 4
♣ ---

East

♠ ---
♡ 10
♢ K 3 2
♣ ---

South

♠ ---
♡ J
♢ A 10 9
♣ ---

Hearts are trump!

South should lead the ♡J to dummy's ace. This accomplishes two things.

First, South draws the out- standing enemy trump, and second, South wants the lead in dummy in order to take the diamond finesse.

South hopes that East has the ♢K and that he can trap it between the dummy and his own hand. To that purpose, he must first lead one of dummy's honors, either the queen or jack. If the finesse wins, he wants to stay in dummy to repeat it.

If he first leads the ♢5, the finesse will win but he will be unable to repeat it and East will still score his king.

2.

North

♠ A Q
♡ 10 9
♢ ---
♣ ---

West

♠ K 7
♡ 4 2
♢ ---
♣ ---

East

♠ J 5
♡ Q 8
♢ ---
♣ ---

South

♠ 8 4
♡ K J
♢ ---
♣ ---

There is no trump suit!

South should play dummy's ♠Q. If West has the king (he does) the queen will win the trick.

When South plays hearts, he wants the first lead to come from dummy. He hopes that East has the ♡Q and can be finessed out of it.

To that end, he leads the ♡10 off dummy and when East follows low, he inserts the jack from his hand. Because East has the ♡Q and has already played a losing card (to the trick in progress) West cannot win the trick and the finesse wins.

3. Clubs are trump.

South is on lead and wants to win 3 out of 4 tricks.

What card should South lead first?

If South leads a small club and West follows low, which card should be played from dummy and why?

If South wants to win a heart trick, which hand must lead the first heart, his or dummy's?

4. Diamonds are trump.

South is on lead and wants to score 3 out of 4 tricks. Which card should he lead first?

Assume South leads the ♠7 and West follows low, what card should South play from dummy?

Do you see why South didn't draw the opponents' trump immediately?

3.

North
♠ ---
♡ 7 5
♢ ---
♣ Q 10

West
♠ ---
♡ J 10
♢ ---
♣ J 8

East
♠ ---
♡ K 8
♢ ---
♣ 9 2

South
♠ ---
♡ Q 2
♢ ---
♣ 4 3

4.

North
♠ A J 10
♡ ---
♢ J
♣ ---

West
♠ K 6 5
♡ ---
♢ 6
♣ ---

East
♠ Q 3
♡ ---
♢ 10
♣ A--

South
♠ 9 8 7
♡ ---
♢ K
♣ ---

Analysis:

3.

North
♠ ---
♡ 7 5
♢ ---
♣ Q 10

West
♠ ---
♡ J 10
♢ ---
♣ J 8

East
♠ ---
♡ K 8
♢ ---
♣ 9 2

South
♠ ---
♡ Q 2
♢ ---
♣ 4 3

Clubs are trump!

South should lead a small club. After West follows low, South hopes he has the ♣J and finesses dummy's 10. When the finesse wins, South finishes drawing the opponents' trump by cashing the ♣Q.

South first played clubs for two reasons. He wanted to draw the outstanding trump and he wanted to enter the dummy to lead a heart toward his high card, the ♡Q.

Now that he's in the dummy, he leads a small heart, hoping that East has the king. He does, and no matter which card East follows with, declarer's queen must win a trick.

4.

North
♠ A J 10
♡ ---
♢ J
♣ ---

West
♠ K 6 5
♡ ---
♢ 6
♣ ---

East
♠ Q 3
♡ ---
♢ 10
♣ A

South
♠ 9 8 7
♡ ---
♢ K
♣ ---

Diamonds are trump!

South must lead a small spade. He is going to take a double finesse, hoping that West has at least 1 of the missing spade honors. Notice that even if West held both of them, South still must lose 1 spade trick.

When West follows low, South plays dummy's 10 (or jack) which loses to East's queen. East cannot now play the ♠A, because South will trump it on dummy, throwing his spade loser from hand. East, therefore, returns a trump to South's king. It was for this very reason that South didn't draw the outstanding trump; he needed an entry back to his hand to repeat the spade finesse and he needed his trump to protect against the ♠A.

COMING UP:

Simple Overcalls

Instant Glossary

Communication:	The art of crossing from hand to hand. Sometimes called transportation.
Entry:	A winning card which allows access to the opposite hand. Does not have to be an immediate winner.
Finesse:	An attempt to render an opponent's high card worthless by playing for it to be in a favorable position. A 50% chance of winning an extra trick.
Double Finesse:	An attempt to devalue 2 high cards held by the opponents by taking two finesses in the same suit. In cases where the 2 high cards are in sequence, the declarer can win at most 1 extra trick.

Instant Glossary

Void: (---)	Whenever you have no cards in any given suit, you are "void" in that suit.
Singleton:	Only 1 card in any given suit.
Doubleton:	Only 2 cards in any given suit.
Tripleton:	3 cards in any given suit.

Instant Glossary

| Stopper: | A protected honor card. |

| Solid suit: | A long suit (at least 5 cards) which usually plays for no losers. |

| Semi-solid suit: | A long suit which usually plays for 1 or 2 losers at most. |

| Quick tricks: | Honor cards or a combination of honor cards which almost always win tricks, whether you are declaring or defending. |

Instant Glossary

Pre-empt:

An obstructive bid made on a high level which makes it difficult for the opponents to enter the auction.

Sometimes called a shut-out bid.

Broken suit:

A long suit which normally plays for more than 2 losers.

Playable suit:

Usually a long suit (5 or more) always headed by at least the queen and jack.

Sacrifice:

Deliberately bidding to a contract you do not expect to make, in order to prevent the opponents from scoring their own contract.

Ruff or Ruffing:

To trump or trumping.

As you continue to play bridge on a regular basis, you know that while one side may open the bidding, the other side may have most of the high cards.

In fact, even if one side opens, their opponents may have enough trick-taking values to bid and make a game.

To find out, the opponents must enter the auction and communicate just like the opener and responder.

They do so by calling over an opening bid.

When one side bids after the other has opened, it's called an overcall.

Overcalling is essential to becoming a good bridge player.

Overcalling is similar to "regular" bidding. Once you learn the requirements, begin putting them to use immediately.

You wouldn't want the opponents to "steal" a contract when the hand belongs to you, and don't depend on their silence when your side opens.

Competitive bidding is a challenging and exciting dimension of bridge. Now either side, regardless of who opens, can compete for the contract.

This chapter will present the rules for simple overcalling. Make sure you understand them, because you will want to compete in as many auctions as your hand permits.

Notes:

Explanation:

The bidding continues to move in a clockwise direction and any bid (other than pass) must be higher than the previous bid.

If an opponent opens 1♠, your side cannot overcall with 1♡. To enter the auction in hearts, you must bid at least 2♡.

The auction is over only when three players in a row have passed, or when no one can open, which requires four passes.

An overcall may be made with fewer points than an opening bid.

To compensate, the overcaller tends to guarantee a playable suit, 5 cards or longer in length. This is true whether that suit is a minor or a major.

When you overcall a suit at the one level, you promise at least 9 points and a playable 5-card suit.

South opens 1◊, and as West you speak next:

<u>West</u> (10)

♠ K Q 10 8 7 5
♡ A J
◊ 9 7
♣ 10 8 5

Overcall 1♠. You meet the pointcount requirement and you have a good 6-card suit.

You wouldn't open the bidding with this hand, but 10 points is enough to overcall.

When you overcall a suit on the
two level, you promise a
minimum of 12 points and a
playable 5-card suit.

South opens 1♦, and as West you
speak next:

West (12)

♠ 7 5
♡ Q J 9 8 6 4
♦ A K J
♣ J 8

Overcall 2♡. If partner has a
fit and enough points, you may
even have game.

Never overcall a suit on the two
level when you can bid it on the
one level.

South opens 1♡, and as West you
speak next:

West (13)

♠ A K J 6 4
♡ K 3 2
♦ J 5 4
♣ J 6

Overcall 1♠. Although you meet
the requirements for overcalling
on the two level, the correct
action is to bid your suit on the
one level.

If partner has a strong hand, the
bidding is still low. This
leaves more room to explore for
the best spot.

And if partner has a bad hand,
you will be in less danger on
the one level.

When you overcall 1NT, you must
meet all requirements for a 1NT
opening bid.

Notes:

If you only have three suits stopped, you guarantee protection in any suit which has been bid by the opponents.

South opens 1♡, and as West you speak next:

West (17)

♠ J 8 5
♡ A Q 10
◇ K J 8 4
♣ K Q J

Overcall 1NT. Only three suits are stopped, but one of them is hearts, the opener's suit.

If West were the dealer, he would open 1NT.

When you overcall a suit by pre-empting to a high level, you must meet all the requirements of an opening pre-empt.

South opens 1♡, and as West you speak next:

West (7)

♠ K Q J 9 8 7 4
♡ 6
◇ J 8 4 3
♣ 7

Overcall 3♠. You would have opened the bidding by pre-empting 3♠, and the fact that an opponent opened in front of you should not be a deterent.

Do not overcall when you have great length and/or strength in a suit bid by the opponents.

South opens 1◇, and as West you speak next:

Notes:

<u>West</u> (12)

♠ 9 8 6
♡ A J
♢ A K 10 8 5
♣ 7 5 3

Pass. When you have excessive
values in a suit bid by the
opponents, it's better to pass
and await developments.

If the opposition plays in
diamonds, you may defeat them
badly, even on the one level.

There is no set rule which
establishes when you have too
many of the opponent's suit to
bid.

In general, do not overcall when
you think you can defeat a
contract with their suit as
trump.

If partner can enter the auction
on his own, you will have a
chance to bid later.

Explanation:

After your partner overcalls,
respond as if he had opened the
bidding. There are only a few
exceptions.

When your partner overcalls, show
a fit as usual, with as few as
6 points.

South opens 1♣ and partner
overcalls 1♠. After North
passes, you speak next:

<u>East</u> (7)

♠ J 9 4
♡ K 6 4 3
♢ Q J 10 2
♣ 9 4

Bid 2♠. You are responding as if

Notes:

partner had opened 1♠ instead of overcalling.

By raising partner's suit one level, you show a fit and a minimum response.

If your point count were 12 to 15, you would have skipped over a level and bid 3♠. This shows a fit and an intermediate response.

When partner overcalls, bid a new suit on the one level with a minimum of 8 points and a playable suit.

This is an exception to normal responding rules. Partner can have as few as 9 points so you want to be more cautious.

South opens 1◊ and partner overcalls 1♡. After North passes, you speak next:

<u>East</u> (7)

♠ K J 9 8
♡ 8 6
◊ J 7 4
♣ Q 5 3 2

Pass. With no fit in hearts and only 7 points you are too weak to suggest a new suit.

If partner has a bare 9 points, any further bidding will only lead to trouble.

If he has a strong hand, you should get another chance to bid.

When partner overcalls, bid a new suit on the two level (or higher) with 10 or more points and a minimum of 5 cards in your suit.

You would not, however, bid your suit on the two level if you could bid it on the one level.

Exactly as if your partner had opened.

South opens 1◊ and partner over-calls 1♧. After North passes, you speak next:

<u>East</u> (11)

♧ 7 5
♡ K Q 2
◊ 4 3
♧ A Q 10 6 4 2

Bid 2♧. You have a good hand and are taking the first step toward exploring for a possible game.

When partner overcalls, bid no trump with the correct point count and no other available bid.

Again, this is exactly the same as responding to an opening bid.

The only difference is that partner may have 9 points instead of the 13 needed to open.

If he does have a minimum in terms of high cards, notrump may prove to be a dangerous under-taking.

So you take out insurance by making your point count requirements more restrictive:

Bid 1NT with 8 to 12 points.
Bid 2NT with 13 to 15 points.

These point counts are higher then those needed to respond to an opening bid and therefore provide an extra margin of safety.

Notes:

You are also required to have a sure stopper or stoppers in any suit bid by the opponents.

South opens 1◇ and partner overcalls 1♡. After North passes, you speak next:

East (9)

♠ J 9 7
♡ J 7
◇ A 10 8 3
♣ Q J 8 4

Bid 1NT. This denies a fit, shows no available bid and 8 to 12 points.

Without the ♣Q you would pass as your hand would contain fewer than 8 points.

South opens 1◇ and partner overcalls 1♡. After North passes, you speak next:

East (13)

♠ A 10 9
♡ J 7
◇ A J 10 6
♣ Q J 8 4

Bid 2NT. This time you have no fit and an intermediate hand, 13 to 15 points.

You also have two stoppers in diamonds, the opponent's bid suit.

Generally, when you jump in notrump in response to an overcall, you promise two stoppers in any suit bid by the opponents.

If your holding in opener's suit suggests that you can win two tricks, you have a double stopper.

When partner overcalls 1NT, respond exactly as if he had opened 1NT:

With fewer than 8 points, pass.

With 8 or 9 points, invite to game by bidding 2NT.

With 10 points or more, bid 3NT.

When partner overcalls by pre-empting to a high level, you need the same number of quick tricks to bid game as if he had opened a pre-empt:

With a minimum of 4 1/2 quick tricks raise partner's major suit to game.

With a minimum of 5 1/2 quick tricks raise partner's minor suit to game.

New bids:

When partner overcalls, bid 3NT with 16 or more points and at least two stoppers in any suit bid by the opposition.

Bid game in partner's major suit with 16 or more points and a fit.

The reason is simple. Bid game if you know you have a good chance to make it.

If you just bid 2NT or 3 of partner's major, he will pass with a minimum point count.

If partner had opened the bidding with one in a suit, he could not pass these jump responses.

Notes:

Even a minimum opening of 13 points will usually produce a game opposite an intermediate response.

So the opening bidder will not pass once the responder announces an intermediate point count.

But the overcaller will pass an intermediate response with minimum value for his overcall.

So if partner overcalls and you think you have game, you must bid it!

Finally, when partner overcalls and the next opponent bids, make sure you have a good reason for entering the auction.

Both opponents have announced positive values and they will be quick to exact penalties if you step out of line.

You can always show a fit with as few as 6 points, but if you bid anything else (other than pass) you must have quick tricks and not just random points.

This completes simple overcalls. There is only one special bid which remains to be explained: the take-out or informative double and it will be covered shortly.

First, bid the problem hands which appear on the following page.

You no longer will bid both hands belonging to the partnership. You will make only the overcaller's initial bid.

Review the explanations if you answer a problem incorrectly.

A quick review:

Whenever you bid after the other side has opened, it's called an overcall. Your partner can respond to your overcall.

In other words, there may be two responders, one for the opener and one for the overcaller.

To overcall a suit on the one level, you need 9 or more points and a playable 5-card suit.

To overcall a suit on the two level, you promise at least 12 points and a playable 5-card suit.

To overcall 1NT or pre-empt to a high level, you must meet all requirements necessary to open with these bids.

Do not overcall when one of the opponents has bid your suit. Pass and see what happens.

In general, respond to an overcall as if it were an opening bid. If you cannot remember the exceptions, go back and review them now.

South opens the bidding with 1◊. You are West and speak next.
What action do you take with each of the 12 hands presented
below? Do you pass or overcall? Point count continues to be
supplied within the parentheses ().

1. (10)

♠ K Q J 6 5
♡ A 3
◊ 9 6 5
♣ 7 6 5

_____

2. (17)

♠ K J 3
♡ A 2
◊ Q J 9 8
♣ A Q 3 2

_____

3. (10)

♠ Q J 7 6 4
♡ A J 10 8
◊ 7 5 3
♣ Q

_____

4. (16)

♠ A J 10
♡ K J 9 8
◊ A J 9
♣ Q 9 4

_____

5. (13)

♠ 8 7 4
♡ K 2
◊ J 8
♣ A K Q 9 5 2

_____

6. (6)

♠ 8 7
♡ K Q J 7 6 5 4
◊ 10
♣ 10 9 8

_____

7. (8)

♠ J 8 7 6
♡ J 7
◊ 10 8
♣ K Q J 10 3

_____

8. (12)

♠ K 6 4
♡ 8 6 5
◊ A K Q 3 2
♣ 10 7

_____

9. (17)

♠ 8 5 4
♡ K Q 4
◊ A Q J
♣ A J 5 3

_____

10. (10)

♠ K Q 3
♡ Q J 10 5 4
◊ Q 3
♣ 10 8 7

_____

11. (6)

♠ 9 8 5
♡ A Q 10 9 8
◊ 8 7
♣ 8 7 3

_____

12. (11)

♠ K Q J 10
♡ A J 4 3 2
◊ 7 6 3
♣ 6

_____

Answers:

1.   Overcall 1♠ (161).

2.   Overcall 1NT (162, 163).

3.   Overcall 1♠ (161).

4.   Overcall 1NT (162, 163).

5.   Overcall 2♠ (162).

6.   Overcall 3♡. This is a pre-empt (163).

7.   Pass. You have only 8 points (162).

8.   Pass. Your suit is diamonds, the opener's suit (163, 164).

9.   Overcall 1NT (162, 163).

10.   Overcall 1♡ (161).

11.   Pass. You have only 6 points (161).

12.   Overcall 1♡ (161).

COMING UP:

A Special Overcall

The Take-Out Double

In bridge, there is one bid which has two different meanings, depending on how and when it is applied.

The bid is the double.

The most obvious application occurs when you feel reasonably sure that you can defeat the opponents' contract.

You would then double them for penalties, and if in fact you did defeat them, you would receive extra points in the scoring.

This is called a penalty double and you will see how it affects point totals in the chapter on scoring.

However, a double is not always for penalty. This bid is available to the overcaller as a tool for sending and receiving information that no other bid will supply.

When the overcaller doubles for information, it is called a take-out double.

Because a double can have two different meanings, it is the most complicated bid for the beginner to use with any degree of confidence.

But you must be comfortable with it before you can play good bridge.

If you have any trouble understanding the usage of the take-out double as opposed to the penalty double, reread this chapter before going any further.

New terms:

Penalty double: A double which states that you think the opponents will not make their contract.

Take-out double: Sometimes called an informative double, it is usually made on a low level and asks partner to bid his longest suit.

Cue bid: When you or your partner bids a suit which was first mentioned by one of the opponents, it is called a cue bid.

You are "cue bidding" an opponent's suit.

A cue bid forces partner to keep bidding until the partnership reaches a game or slam.

Explanation:

The overcaller may employ the take-out double whenever his hand is rich in high cards without a 5-card suit to bid.

South opens 1♣, and as West you speak next:

West (14)

♠ K Q J 4
♡ Q J 9 8
♢ A J 4 2
♣ 7

You would like to compete, but in spite of your 14 points, you have no bid.

You cannot overcall 1♢, 1♡ or 1♠ because none are 5-card suits and when you overcall a suit you always promise at least 5 cards in it.

But if you pass, the chances are that partner will be unable to enter the auction on his own.

It appears that either you mislead partner about your suit length, or pass tamely and allow the opponents an unimpeded auction when it may be your hand.

But there is another choice: you can double.

This double is for take-out and askes partner to bid his longest suit.

In order to add the double to your bidding arsenal, you must know when your double will be interpreted for take-out as opposed to penalty.

Record your auctions like this:

Use compass abbreviations for each player's position and suit symbols or abbreviations for each bid.

For example, south is the dealer:

S	W	N	E
1♡	1♠	3♡	P
4♡	P	P	P

The abbreviation for the dealer, in this case South, is always written first. The other players follow in normal clockwise order.

South opened 1♡, West over-called 1♠, North jumped to 3♡ and South bid the game.

P stands for pass.
Use capital D to signify a double, either take-out or penalty.

Obviously, you can't say "This double is for take-out" or "This double is penalty."

Nor would it be ethical to convey information through vocal intonation.

You are not allowed to bid one double with an exclamation point (DOUBLE!) and the other with a question mark (double?).

By using each double in its proper place, partner will recognize which kind of double it is.

When your double will be understood as take-out:

> If the auction is still on the one or two level, and partner has not bid (other than pass) your double is take-out.

> If you double at your first opportunity it is take-out.

> Take-out doubles are usually made on a low level, with one exception. If the opener pre-empts on the three level, your double is still take-out.

All other doubles tend to be penalty.

When your double will be understood as penalty:

> If the opponents reach a contract on the three level or higher, you double for penalty if you think they can be defeated.

Notes:

The exception is an opening pre-empt on the three level.

If partner has made a bid (other than pass), your double is penalty regardless of the level.

If you double after your first opportunity to do so, it is penalty.

All other doubles tend to be for take-out.

Now that you know how your double will be interpreted, your hand must meet certain requirements before you can double for take-out.

Double for take-out when you have opening bid values plus shortness in any suit bid by the opposition and some support for any suit partner may bid.

Remember, your double forces partner to bid and he may have a bad hand. To avoid danger, you should have at least 3-card support for any suit partner may bid.

South opens 1♣. As West, you would double for take-out with any of these hands:

A take-out double asks partner to bid his longest suit.

In most cases he must bid, even with no points.

1. <u>West</u> (14)

  ♠ A J 9 7
  ♡ Q J 9 4
  ◇ K Q J 2
  ♣ 5

2. <u>West</u> (15)

  ♠ A K Q J
  ♡ 10 8 5 4
  ◇ K Q 2
  ♣ 6 4

3. <u>West</u> (14)

  ♠ A Q J 6
  ♡ A K 8 5
  ◇ 10 9 8 7
  ♣ 8

4. <u>West</u> (14)

  ♠ Q 10 9 5
  ♡ A K J
  ◇ K 10 8 6
  ♣ J 4

Hands 1 and 3 are considered "classic" take-out doubles. They have extreme shortness in the opener's suit and at least 4-card support for any suit partner chooses to bid.

Double for take-out whenever you want information from partner, even with a 5-card suit.

You are still obligated to hold opening bid values and shortness in any suit bid by the opposition.

South opens 1◊. As West, you would double for take-out with any of these hands:

1. <u>West</u> (14
   ♠ K 9 8 7 6
   ♡ A K 3
   ◊ 10
   ♣ A 8 4 3

2. <u>West</u> (15)
   ♠ A J 10
   ♡ K Q J 3
   ◊ 6
   ♣ K J 9 8 7

3. <u>West</u> (13)
   ♠ Q J 9 8
   ♡ A K 5 3
   ◊ ---
   ♣ K 5 4 3 2

4. <u>West</u> (13)
   ♠ A 9 8 2
   ♡ Q J 5 4 2
   ◊ 8
   ♣ A Q 10

With each of these hands you could overcall your 5-card suit, but it is more flexible to double.

You want partner to know about your opening bid values, and you have support for any suit he may bid.

Always try to make the bid which gives partner the most information.

Clearly, a take-out double says much more than an overcall.

Notes:

Double for take-out whenever your hand contains 17 or more points and is unsuitable for an overcall of 1NT.

You still need shortness in any suit bid by the opponents, but you are no longer required to hold support for any suit partner may bid.

Even if you hold a very long suit (6 cards or longer) double before you bid it.

Remember, an overcall may show as few as 9 points. If partner passes with some values, you could miss a game.

By doubling, you keep the bidding open because you force partner to name his longest suit. When you subsequently bid your own suit, partner will wonder why you didn't overcall.

He will know that you had to double first to show a strong hand. Now he is better equipped to gauge whether the partnership has a game.

In short:

When you double for take-out and then bid your own suit, you promise a minimum of 17 points and a playable 5-card (or longer) suit.

South opens 1◊. As West, you would double for take-out with any of these hands:

1. <u>West</u> (18)
   ♠ A K J 8 6 4
   ♡ K Q 4
   ◊ K 3
   ♣ Q 10

2. <u>West</u> (17)
   ♠ A K
   ♡ Q J 10 7 5
   ◊ K 10
   ♣ A 9 8 3

Notes:

3. West (19)   4. West (18)

♠ A Q   ♠ K J 8
♡ A K Q 4 3 2 ♡ A 4
♢ A 2   ♢ 4 3 2
♣ 7 6 4   ♣ A K Q J 3

With each of these hands you would double first and then bid your suit. The danger in making a simple overcall is that partner may believe you to have considerably fewer points than you actually have.

By doubling first and then bidding your suit, he will know you have a strong hand.

Do not double for take-out when you have excessive length and/or strength in a suit bid by the opponents.

South opens 1♡, and as West you speak next:

West (18)

♠ K Q J
♡ A K J 9 6
♢ Q J
♣ J 3 2

Pass. You would like to double for penalty but partner will read it as take-out and will bid his longest suit.

That is the last thing you want.

But if you keep quiet, the opponents may settle in a heart contract.

That is exactly what you want.

When you think that you can defeat a contract with an opponent's suit as trump, you should be defending and not declaring.

A quick review:

A double is for take-out:

If the auction is still on the one or two level, and partner has not made a bid, other than pass.

If you double at your first opportunity to do so.

If the opener has pre-empted on the three level.

A take-out double promises:

Opening bid values.

Shortness in any suit bid by the opposition.

Good support for the unbid suits.

Or else, any hand which contains 17 or more points and is unsuitable for an overcall of 1NT.

Do not double for take-out:

When you have excessive length and/or strength in a suit bid by the opponents.

BIDDING BOX!

South opens the bidding with 1♡. As West, you speak next. What action do you take with each of the 12 hands presented below? Do you pass, overcall or double for take-out?

---

1. (10)

♠ A K J 9 8
♡ J 8
♢ J 9 8 5
♣ 7 6

_____

2. (14)

♠ K Q 5 4 3
♡ 8
♢ A J 10 9
♣ K J 6

_____

3. (17)

♠ K Q J 10 9 8
♡ Q 3
♢ K J
♣ A J 5

_____

4. (7)

♠ K Q J 9 8 7 6
♡ 8 5
♢ J 6 5
♣ 7

_____

5. (18)

♠ A Q J
♡ K J 8
♢ K Q 4 3
♣ Q 4 3

_____

6. (13)

♠ 8 6 5
♡ A K J 10 9
♢ K Q 4
♣ 4 3

_____

7. (14)

♠ K J 8 7
♡ 7
♢ A Q J 10
♣ K 9 7 5

_____

8. (12)

♠ J 8 7
♡ 9
♢ K Q 3
♣ K Q J 9 8 5

_____

9. (14)

♠ Q J 8 7
♡ J 8
♢ A K J
♣ Q 10 4 3

_____

10. (18)

♠ A K
♡ 8 5
♢ A Q J 9 6 4
♣ A 5 3

_____

11. (13)

♠ A J 8 7
♡ 8
♢ 10 9 8 7 6
♣ A K J

_____

12. (12)

♠ K Q 10
♡ 7 5
♢ 9 8
♣ A Q J 10 6 3

_____

Answers:

1.   Overcall 1♠ (161).

2.   Double. An overcall of 1♠ is acceptable, but double is better. You don't wnat to suggest spades when you can find your best spot by doubling (176).

3.   Double. With 17 points you double first, bid your suit later (178).

4.   Overcall 3♠. This is a pre-empt (163).

5.   Overcall 1NT (162, 163).

6.   Pass. You have the opener's suit (hearts)   (163, 174 & 179).

7.   Double. This is a classic take-out double (176).

8.   Overcall 2♠ (162).

9.   Double. You want to know partner's longest suit (176).

10. Double. With 18 points double first, bid your suit later (178).

11. Double. You want to know partner's longest suit (176).

12. Overcall 2♠ (162).

Explanation:

When partner doubles for take-out, it is a request for you to bid your longest **suit.**

If the next opponent passes, you must bid because it may be dangerous not to.

Remember:

Partner's double suggests shortness in the suit he doubled. If you pass his take-out double, you allow the opposition to play in a suit you know partner to be short in.

And you may allow them to play at a safe level when your side should be declaring.

Therefore, respond to partner's take-out double, even with no points.

When partner doubles for take-out, bid your suit on the lowest possible level with 0 to 9 points; skip over one level with 10 to 12 points.

South is the dealer:

<u>S</u>	<u>W</u>	<u>N</u>	<u>E</u>
1◊	D	P	??

As East, you must respond to partner's take-out double. Bid 1♠ with these hands:

1. **East** (0)   2. **East** (5)

♠ 8 7 5 3   ♠ J 10 5 4
♡ 8 5 4   ♡ 6 2
◊ 10 5 4 2   ◊ A 4 3 2
♣ 10 9   ♣ 9 8 7

And 2♠ with these hands:

3. **East (11)**

    ♠ K Q 4 3
    ♡ A 2
    ◇ Q 5 4 3
    ♣ 8 5 2

4. **East (12)**

    ♠ J 10 9 8
    ♡ A Q 10
    ◇ 4 2
    ♣ K Q 10 8

With hands 1 and 2, you are telling partner that your hand is weak and to proceed at his own risk.

With hands 3 and 4, you promise a chance for game by skipping over one level.

Notice that in each hand, East has two 4-card suits. You should strain to bid a major because major suit games require one less trick than minor suit games. And even if you stop below game, major suit contracts score more than minor suit contracts bid on the same level.

When partner doubles for take-out, cue bid an opponent's suit if you have enough points to play game in a major or minor suit.

A cue bid usually promises at least 13 points and a desire to play in game.

South opens 1◇ and partner doubles. After North passes, you speak next:

1. **East (14)**

    ♠ K Q 4 3
    ♡ A Q 4 3
    ◇ J 5
    ♣ Q 10 8

2. **East (15)**

    ♠ A J 10 9
    ♡ K Q 8 5
    ◇ 9 8 7
    ♣ A J

With these hands, you should cue bid 2◇.

Partner has shown opening bid values and support for the unbid suits. You almost surely have a major suit fit and enough points for game.

A warning to the take-out doubler:

When you double for take-out, you force partner to bid if the next opponent passes-- even with no points.

If he bids one of your suits without skipping a level, be very careful before you raise him to a higher level.

Good support is not enough reason to raise. If partner has a poor hand, even the two level may be too high.

You should have at least 16 points before raising his suit one level, and at least 19 points before you raise his suit by skipping over a level.

A cue bid will prevent partner from passing until you have reached your best game contract.

When partner doubles for take-out, cue bid if your hand promises a good chance for game, even without 13 points.

South opens 1◇ and partner doubles. After North passes, you speak next:

East (10)

♠ A Q 7 6 4
♡ K J 10 8 7
◇ 8
♣ 10 9

Cue bid 2◇, even though you have only 10 points.

The odds are excellent that your partnership has a game in a major suit. The cue bid will keep the bidding open until you reach it.

The two five-card major suits and your trumping value in the minors more than compensate for the missing high card points.

When partner doubles for take-out, respond in notrump with good stoppers in any suit bid by the opposition and the correct point count:

Bid 1NT with 6 to 9 points.

Bid 2NT with 10 to 12 points.

Bid 3NT with 13 points or more.

Notes:

Remember:

You guarantee a solid stopper in the opponents' suit.

If you are going to bid 2NT or 3NT you should have at least two stoppers in any suit bid by the opposition.

South opens 1♡ and partner doubles. After North passes, you speak next:

1. <u>East</u> (8)
   - ♠ K 2
   - ♡ Q J 2
   - ◇ Q 4 3 2
   - ♣ 10 9 8 7

2. <u>East</u> (9)
   - ♠ J 7
   - ♡ K 8 5 4
   - ◇ Q 10 9
   - ♣ Q J 5 3

3. <u>East</u> (11)
   - ♠ Q J 7
   - ♡ K J 10 8
   - ◇ K 6 4 3
   - ♣ J 9

4. <u>East</u> (14)
   - ♠ K J 8
   - ♡ A Q J
   - ◇ K 7 6 4
   - ♣ 9 8 5

With hands 1 and 2, bid 1NT.

With hand 3, bid 2NT.

With hand 4, bid 3NT. Even though you have 14 points, you do not cue bid because your hand is suitable for play in notrump.

You do not have to explore when you know which contract will provide the best play for game.

If partner has a long suit, he can always bid it over your 3NT.

When partner doubles for take-out, you are no longer obligated to respond if the next opponent makes a bid other than pass.

You should have a good hand, at least 7 points, before you enter the auction.

Notes:

After all, one opponent has announced 13 points or better and the other opponent has enough points to respond.

Be very careful when you know the opposition holds a majority of the points.

When partner doubles for take-out and the next opponent passes, you can pass if you are sure you can defeat a low level contract with that suit as trump.

This is the only time you can pass partner's take-out double. But you should be positive that this action will produce your best score.

This is called converting your partner's take-out double to penalty.

South opens 1◊ and partner doubles. After North passes, you speak next:

1. __East__ (9)   2. __East__ (8)

♠ J 7   ♠ 6 4 3
♡ 8 5 4   ♡ 8 5 4
◊ A Q J 9 8 6   ◊ A K J 9 8 7
♣ J 6   ♣ 5

With either of these hands, pass. You want to play with diamonds as trump and you expect to beat the opponents by at least two or three tricks.

Furthermore, it is very unlikely that your side can score a contract with another suit as trump.

Be very careful before you convert partner's take-out double into penalty. Partner may lose confidence in your judgment if the opponents score their contract.

Explanation:

When it is partner who opens the bidding and an **OPPONENT** who makes a take-out double, respond normally to your partner.

With 6 or more points you can show a fit, suggest a new suit or bid notrump with no other available bid.

New bid:

After partner opens and the next opponent doubles for take-out, you can redouble with 10 or more points.*

Redouble tends to deny a fit with partner's suit.

West, your partner, is the dealer:

<u>W</u>	<u>N</u>	<u>E</u>	<u>S</u>
1♡	D	RD	P

RD is the abbreviation for redouble. After partner opens, North doubles and you redouble.

This announces a good hand without a fit in hearts.

Partner now knows that your side has the majority of high cards. He has been alerted to game possibilities and will be quick to double for penalties if the opposition steps out of line.

* A redouble has a different meaning if the opponents doubled you for penalty. It will be examined in the chapter on scoring.

Notes:

Finally:

You cannot double, either for take-out or for penalty, unless the last bid other than pass has been made by an opponent.

You can never open the bidding with a double nor can you double your own partner.

You can never redouble except over an opponent's double and then only if partner has not bid a suit or notrump in between.

This concludes the chapter on take-out doubles. Make sure you understand them and are ready to use them before reading any further.

A quick review:

When partner doubles for take-out:

You must bid if the next opponent passes.

Bid your suit on the lowest possible level with 0 to 9 points.

Skip a level with 10 to 12 points.

Cue bid whenever you want to be in game.

Bid notrump with solid stoppers in any suit bid by the opponents.

    1NT with 6 to 9 points.
    2NT with 10 to 12 points.
    3NT with 13 or more points.

If partner doubles for take-out and the next opponent bids (other than pass) you need at least 7 points to enter the auction.

If partner opens and an opponent doubles for take-out:

Respond normally with 6 or more points.

Redouble with 10 or more points and no fit in partner's suit.

South opens 1◊ and West (your partner) doubles for take-out.
After North passes, you speak next. Decide on what action
you would take with each of the example hands presented below.
Remember, you are responding to a take-out double.

---

1. (4)

♠ K 5 3 2
♡ 8 7 5
◊ J 7
♣ 9 6 5 4

_____

2. (13)

♠ K Q 2
♡ 4 2
◊ A Q J 6
♣ J 10 9 4

_____

3. (11)

♠ J 8
♡ K Q 10 8
◊ 4 3 2
♣ A J 3 2

_____

4. (11)

♠ A K Q 5 4
♡ Q 4 3
◊ 8 6 5
♣ 4 3

_____

5. (1)

♠ 9 6 5
♡ J 8
◊ 5 4 3 2
♣ 9 6 4 3

_____

6. (12)

♠ Q J 10
♡ 5
◊ A K Q 9 8 6
♣ 8 3 2

_____

7. (7)

♠ K 3 2
♡ 6 4
◊ K J 8
♣ 9 8 7 5 4

_____

8. (10)

♠ K Q J 5 4
♡ A 10 9 8 7
◊ 8
♣ 3 2

_____

9. (11)

♠ 3 2
♡ K J 8
◊ A J 9 8
♣ Q 10 5 4

_____

10. (14)

♠ K Q 4 3
♡ A J 8 5 3
◊ 8
♣ K J 7

_____

11. (11)

♠ K Q 3
♡ A 2
◊ 8 7 2
♣ Q 9 8 5 3

_____

12. (1)

♠ 9 8 5 4
♡ 9 6 5 3
◊ 7 4
♣ J 10 9

_____

Answers:

1. Bid 1♠ (182).

2. Bid 3NT (184).

3. Bid 2♡. With two four-card suits, you should bid the major suit first (182, 183).

4. Bid 2♠ (182).

5. Bid 2♣ (182).

6. Pass. You expect to defeat 1◇ by at least 2 or 3 tricks and this will probably be your optimum result (186).

7. Bid 1NT. You could bid 2♣, but partner will think that you may have no value at all (see hand 5). In order to tell him that you have some points as well as a stopper in the opener's suit, bid 1NT (184).

    Even though you have 5 clubs, 1NT is still the best bid because it gives partner the most information about your hand.

8. Cue bid 2◇. You do not have the 13 points usually necessary to cue bid, but you expect your hand to produce game in a major suit (183).

9. Bid 2NT (184).

10. Cue bid 2◇. This time you have 14 points and are looking for game in a major suit (183).

11. Bid 3♣. You must skip a level to show 10 to 12 points (182).

12. Bid 1♡. With two four-card majors and a poor hand, bid the lowest suit first (27 & 182).

Play these hands!

1. South is the declarer and there is no trump suit.

    South is on lead and must win all 5 tricks.

    What card should South lead first?

    Assume South leads a spade and wins the trick with dummy's ace.

    What card should South lead to the second trick?

    And the third trick?

2. South is the declarer and hearts are trump.

    South is on lead and must win all 5 tricks.

    What card should South lead first?

    If South wins the first trick with dummy's ◇K, which card should he lead next?

1.

North
♠ A K
♡ ---
♢ ---
♣ 5 3 2

West
♠ Q 9 4
♡ ---
♢ ---
♣ 7 4

East
♠ J 10
♡ ---
♢ ---
♣ K 10 9

South
♠ 7 6
♡ ---
♢ ---
♣ A Q J

2.

North
♠ ---
♡ 5 4 2
♢ K Q
♣ ---

West
♠ ---
♡ 6 3
♢ J 5 3
♣ ---

East
♠ ---
♡ Q 8 7
♢ 9
♣ 10

South
♠ ---
♡ A K J
♢ 7 4
♣ ---

Analysis:

1.

North
♠ A K
♡ ---
♢ ---
♣ 5 3 2

West
♠ Q 9 4
♡ ---
♢ ---
♣ 7 4

East
♠ J 10
♡ ---
♢ ---
♣ K 10 9

South
♠ 7 6
♡ ---
♢ ---
♣ A Q J

There <u>is</u> <u>no</u> <u>trump</u> <u>suit</u>!

South wants to enter dummy to try the club finesse. The only way to dummy is through a spade honor, so at trick one, South leads a small spade to dummy's ace.

South must now try the club finesse immediately, He leads a club off dummy and when East follows low, he successfully finesses the jack.

Next, he must re-enter dummy to repeat the club finesse. His only entry is dummy's ♣K.

If he had cashed the ♣K at trick two, he would have no way of repeating the winning club finesse and would be unable to win all 5 tricks.

2.

North
♠ ---
♡ 5 4 2
♢ K Q
♣ ---

West
♠ ---
♡ 6 3
♢ J 5 3
♣ ---

East
♠ ---
♡ Q 8 7
♢ 9
♣ 10

South
♠ ---
♡ A K J
♢ 7 4
♣ ---

<u>Hearts</u> <u>are</u> <u>trump</u>!

South wants to enter dummy to try the trump finesse. He leads a small diamond to dummy's king.

If he now plays dummy's ♢Q, East will trump it and South will not make his contract. Therefore, he tries the heart finesse first.

He leads dummy's ♡2 and when East follows low he inserts his jack which will win the trick. Next he finishes drawing trump with the ♡A and ♡K and wins the last trick with dummy's ♢Q.

<u>Alternatively</u>, South could cash either the ♡A or ♡K before entering dummy to try the heart finesse.

3. South is the declarer and there is no trump suit.

South is on lead and wants to win all 5 tricks.

What card should South lead first?

Plan the play after West shows out in diamonds.

3.

North
♠ A 8
♡ ---
◇ 5 4 3
♣ ---

West
♠ K Q 6 5
♡ ---
◇ 6
♣ ---

East
♠ 4
♡ ---
◇ J 9 8 7
♣ ---

South
♠ 2
♡ ---
◇ A K Q 10
♣ ---

4. South is the declarer and diamonds are trump.

South is on lead and wants to win all 5 tricks.

South must lead a spade, because that is the only suit he has.

South leads the ♠4 and West discards a small club. What card should South play from dummy and why?

How should South continue?

4.

North
♠ ---
♡ ---
◇ A K J
♣ A K

West
♠ ---
♡ 8
◇ Q 10
♣ J 4

East
♠ ---
♡ ---
◇ 9 8
♣ 8 6 5

South
♠ J 9 8 7 4
♡ ---
◇ ---
♣ ---

Analysis:

3.

North
♠ A 8
♡ ---
♦ 5 4 3
♣ ---

West
♠ K Q 6 5
♡ ---
♦ 6
♣ ---

East
♠ 4
♡ ---
♦ J 9 8 7
♣ ---

South
♠ 2
♡ ---
♦ A K Q 10
♣ ---

There is no trump suit!

South will win every trick if he can score all of his diamonds. If the missing 5 diamonds split with one opponent holding 3 and the other 2, the jack of diamonds will drop and South's 10 will be a winner.

South can also win 4 diamond tricks if the ♦J is singleton.

South starts by cashing the ♦A and ♦K (or ♦Q). When West shows out on the second round, South must cross to dummy and lead a diamond to take the "marked" finesse against East.

If West had held 4 diamonds to the jack, South would be out of luck. He would have to go down in his contract.

4.

North
♠ ---
♡ ---
♦ A K J
♣ A K

West
♠ ---
♡ 8
♦ Q 10
♣ J 4

East
♠ ---
♡ ---
♦ 9 8
♣ 8 6 5

South
♠ J 9 8 7 4
♡ ---
♦ ---
♣ ---

Diamonds are trump!

South must enter dummy to draw the opponent's trump. Once this has been accomplished, all of dummy's remaining cards are winners.

The only way to cross over to dummy is by trumping a spade. South leads a small spade and West discards the ♣4. South must trump with dummy's ♦J.

He knows that both opponents are out of spades and he hopes that East cannot overtrump dummy's jack with the ♦Q. This is a kind of finesse. If West has the ♦Q (he does), then East cannot win the trick. Now South must draw trump or West will ruff the second club honor.

COMING UP:

Hand Evaluation

High Level Bidding

This is the final section on bidding and the most difficult for the beginner to assimilate.

You should not attempt to learn this section in one or even two sittings.

Take your time. Go back and review each individual part until you feel confident with it.

Once you complete it, you will be comfortable playing in almost any game, even with more experienced players.

The areas to be covered are hand evaluation and high level bidding.

Stayman, a method used to reach suit contracts after partner has opened in notrump, will be covered in the appendix and is your first intermediate lesson.

If you want to become a good bridge player, you must be able to compete on an equal basis with other good players.

Begin to practice these principles as soon as possible.

Notes:

Explanation:

There are other factors besides point count which determine the worth of your hand.

Long suits, for example, can be more valuable in regard to trick taking potential than a random assortment of high cards.

And if you find a fit with partner, shortness in other suits can allow you to bid and make a game with fewer high card points than are normally required.

Always consider your suit distribution before deciding what to bid.

You can open the bidding with 12 points if your hand contains a long playable suit or suits and at least 2 quick tricks:

As West you deal and hold:

1.	West (12)	2.	West (12)
	♠ A Q J 9 6		♠ A K J 9 4
	♡ K 10 9 6		♡ Q J 9 6
	◊ Q 9 6		◊ 5
	♣ 7		♣ J 10 9

Open both hands 1♠. Each contains 2 quick tricks and a strong playable suit. Notice that both hands also hold a 4-card heart suit.

This increases their value as it gives partner two chances to find a fit.

You can open the bidding with 11 points only if your hand contains a long playable suit or suits and 3 quick tricks.

As West you deal and hold:

1. <u>West</u> (11)   2. <u>West</u> (11)

  ♠ A K 9 5 4   ♠ A 10 9 8 7
  ♡ 10 8 5   ♡ 9 8 5
  ◇ A 10 9 2   ◇ 6
  ♣ 10   ♣ A K 8 6

Open both hands 1♠. Each hand has 3 quick tricks as well as a long and playable suit.

Be very careful whenever you open an 11 point hand on the one level. Make sure you have a good suit and 3 quick tricks.

Except for a pre-empt, you should never open with fewer than 11 points.

You are not obligated to open if your hand contains exactly 13 points with bad suit quality and under 2 quick tricks.

But 14 points is a mandatory opening.

As West you deal and hold:

1. <u>West</u> (13)   2. <u>West</u> (14)

  ♠ Q J 8   ♠ Q J 8
  ♡ K J   ♡ K J
  ◇ Q 8 6 5 3   ◇ Q J 8 6 5
  ♣ K J 6   ♣ K J 6

Both hands have minimum trick-taking potential for their point count. You are allowed to pass the first hand, but you must open the second with 1◇.

When you and partner find a fit, you can count additional points for shortness outside of the trump suit.

If you open the bidding with an 11- or 12-point hand, treat that hand as a minimum opening throughout the remainder of the auction.

<u>West</u> (12)   <u>East</u> (12)

♠ A 10 4   ♠ J 9
♡ A Q J 9 8   ♡ K 10 7 3
◇ J 10 8   ◇ A 9 3 2
♣ 10 9   ♣ A 6 5

1.   <u>1H</u>   1.   <u>3H</u>
2.   <u>4H</u>   2.   <u>P</u>

West opens 1♡ with only 12 points and after East responds 3♡, West cannot pass. He must continue to treat his hand as a minimum opening bid.

West bids game because a minimum opening opposite an intermediate response almost always produces a good play for game.

Specifically, a void counts 3 points, a singleton 2 points and a doubleton 1 point.

Add these extra points to your high card total and bid accordingly:

West (12)   East (10)

♠ 8 7   ♠ K Q 3 2
♡ K Q 10 9 8   ♡ A J 4 3
♢ A K 10   ♢ 6 5 4 3 2
♣ 10 4 3   ♣ v-o-i-d

1.   1H   1.   3H!
2.   4H   2.   P

After West opens 1♡, East would normally respond 2♡ with only 10 points. However, his hand increases in value because he has a fit with his partner.

East can now add 3 points for the club void and that makes his total count 13 points, enough to make an intermediate response.

When East bids 3♡, West knows about the fit and his value also increases slightly.

West now adds 1 point for the doubleton spade and that makes his total count 13 points.

This time, the added point did not affect West's bidding.

Remember: Never count distributional points unless you have a fit with partner.

A quick review:

You can open the bidding with 12 points if you have a long playable suit or suits and at least 2 quick tricks.

You can open with 11 points if you have a long playable suit or suits and 3 quick tricks.

You are not obligated to open the bidding with exactly 13 points if you have bad suit quality and under 2 quick tricks.

But you must open any 14 point hand.

Once you find a fit, count distributional points for shortness outside of the trump suit: a void = 3 points, a singleton = 2 points and a doubleton = 1 point.

Add these points to your high card total and bid accordingly.

Explanation:

When you and partner bid to the sixth or seventh level you are contracting to win 12 or even all 13 tricks.

These levels pay a bonus for successful completion of your contract, just as game levels do.

The sixth level is called a slam or small slam and the seventh level is called a grand slam.

The bonus for bidding and making a slam or grand slam is more than double and sometimes more than triple a normal game bonus.

Therefore, if your partnership has enough value to bid a slam or grand slam, you must bid it because the rewards are so great for making your contract.

In general, you need at least 33 points between your hand and partner's to bid a slam and at least 37 points to bid a grand slam.

This chapter will examine special strength-showing bids by both the opener and responder, a method of finding out how many aces and kings your partner holds, and slam bidding after partner opens in notrump.

Special strength-showing bids:

Whenever the opener makes a jump shift on his second turn, it shows a minimum of 19 points and suggests the possibility of a slam.

A jump shift by opener always forces the responder to keep the bidding open until a game or

New term:

Jump shift: Whenever opener or responder bids by jumping over one level and shifting into a new suit (not previously mentioned by the partnership) it is called a jump shift.

Here are two examples:

1.	W	E		2.	W	E
	1S	1NT			1H	3C
	3C					

These auctions are incomplete and you should assume that the opponents pass through-out.

In the first auction the opener makes a jump shift and in the second, it is the responder who jump shifts.

slam has been bid by the
partnership.

In general, a jump shift by
opener promises at least 4 cards
in the second bid suit.

West (20)	East (7)
♠ Q 2	♠ A 10 6 5
♡ A K J 9 7	♡ 6 2
◇ A K Q 4	◇ 8 5 3
♣ J 10	♣ K 9 4 3

	West		East
1.	1H	1.	1S
2.	3D	2.	3NT
3.	P	3.	___

West opens 1♡ and East responds
1♠. Now West shows slam
interest by jump shifting into
his second suit, diamonds.

Notice that West did not bid 2◇.
He showed his strength by jumping
over the second level.

East cannot pass his partner's
jump shift. But holding a
minimum response, he has no
thought of slam.

East does not fit either of
West's two suits so he bids the
lowest level game, 3NT.

When the responder jump shifts at
his first opportunity, he commits
the partnership to game and
strongly suggests the possibility
of a slam.

In general, this response shows
either a very strong suit or a
good fit with opener's suit and a
minimum of 18 points.

The reason you would not show a
fit with opener's suit
immediately is that with 18 or
more points your hand is much too
strong for a normal support
showing response.

Notes:

You must first jump shift in another suit, showing slam potential. You can always show your fit for opener's suit later.

West (12)	East (19)
♠ A K 10 6 5	♠ Q J 9 8 6
♡ K Q 9 8	♡ J
◊ 10 8	◊ A K Q 3
♣ 7 5	♣ K Q J

	West			East
1.	1S		1.	3D!
2.	3H		2.	3S
3.	4S		3.	P

After West opens 1♠, East jump shifts by bidding 3◊. He has an excellent spade fit but his hand is too strong for a normal support-showing response.

West now bids his second suit, hearts, and East shows the spade fit.

Notice that East can afford to support spades on the three level. He does not have to bid the game because his jump shift announced at least 18 points and the auction cannot end until the partnership has contracted for a game or slam.

West, however, has a minimum opening and no slam interest. He bids only game, but East can still bid slam if he has a very strong hand for his jump shift.

As you can see, East holds a minimum so he passes his partner's 4♠ bid.

West (12)	East (19)
♠ 7 6	♠ A K Q J 10 9
♡ K Q J 6 5	♡ A 2
◊ A Q 10 9 8	◊ K J
♣ 6	♣ J 3 2

Notes:

1.	1H		1.	2S
2.	3D		2.	3S
3.	4D		3.	4S
4.	6S		4.	P

West opens 1♥ and East jump shifts by bidding 2♠. After West shows his second suit, East repeats his spades.

This confirms that East has a very strong suit as well as at least 18 points.

West now rebids his diamonds because he has more diamonds than he originally promised.

East, however, has no interest in either of his partner's two suits and bids the game in spades.

And now West makes a good decision. With 2-card spade support, he knows that his singleton club will be very valuable to his partner so he bids the slam.

In fact, the singleton club makes the slam almost a sure thing.

Unless an opponent trumps the opening lead (most unlikely) the slam will make.

This kind of slam bidding requires good judgment and judgment can only be developed through playing experience.

As you become a more proficient bridge player, you will develop many techniques to explore for slam.

There is, however, one technique which you can begin to use immediately.

It is an "asking" bid which will enable you to discover exactly how many aces and kings are in

A quick review:

When opener jump shifts on his second turn, he shows 19 or more points, at least 4 cards in the second suit (usually) and a desire to explore for slam.

When responder jump shifts at his first opportunity, he shows either a very strong suit or a good fit with opener's suit and a desire to explore for slam.

All jump shifts commit the partnership to game or slam.

your partner's hand.

Explanation:

When your partnership holds enough points to contract for slam, you will not want to bid it if the opponents can cash two winners before your side gains the lead.

Usually, the only immediate winners that the opponents can cash to defeat your slam are either two aces or an ace and king in the same suit.

Unfortunately, you will not always be able to prevent this from happening, but you can take steps to minimize the risk.

If you are in the slam zone, you can ask partner to tell you how many aces he holds through the use of an artificial bid called Blackwood.

The bid is 4NT.

Whenever the opener or responder bids 4NT* during the auction, he is asking **his** partner for number of aces.

The partner will respond by bidding a suit on the five level, each suit representing a different number of aces:

5♣ means either 0 or all 4 aces.
5◊ means 1 ace.
5♡ means 2 aces.
5♠ means 3 aces.

Remember, the Blackwood bid of 4NT and all responses to it are artificial bids.

> *There are some cases when 4NT will not be Blackwood. The most common exception will be examined shortly.

Notes:

If you bid Blackwood (4NT) inquiring for aces and partner answers 5♣, it does not mean he wishes to play in clubs (though this may be the case). He is simply telling you that he has either 0 or all 4 aces.

Although the 5♣ response to Blackwood may be ambiguous, the Blackwood bidder should know by looking at his own hand whether partner is showing no aces or all 4.

You should use Blackwood when you need to know **that** you don't have two quick losers.

West (19)	East (12)
♠ A K J 9 6 5	♠ Q 4 3 2
♡ K 3 2	♡ A 8 7
◇ K 10	◇ A 3 2
♣ A J	♣ Q 6 4

	West			East
1.	1S		1.	3S
2.	4NT		2.	5H
3.	6S		3.	P

After East announces a fit in spades, West re-asseses his value at 21 points (1 extra point for each doubleton) and knows they are close to slam.

West uses Blackwood (4NT) because he doesn't want to lose two tricks before he can gain the lead.

When East responds 5♡, showing the missing two aces, West knows they are safe and bids the slam.

Once you know the number of partner's aces, you can ask for kings by bidding 5NT.

This bid is made when you think there is a chance for a grand slam.

Notes:

After partner bids 5NT asking for kings, the responses follow the same pattern as for aces:

6♣ means 0 or all 4 kings.
6◊ means 1 king.
6♡ means 2 kings.
6♠ means 3 kings.

You are not allowed to ask for kings until you have first asked for aces.

This means that even if you hold all four aces in your own hand and are only interested in partner's kings, you must still go through the motions of bidding 4NT first.

And whenever you ask for kings, you guarantee that the partnership holds all 4 aces.

West (14)	East (24)
♠ K 6 5	♠ A Q
♡ K Q 8 6 5 4	♡ A J 10 9
◊ K Q 10	◊ A 9 6
♣ J	♣ A K Q 2

	West		East
1.	1H	1.	4NT
2.	5C	2.	5NT
3.	6S	3.	7H
4.	P	4.	___

After West opens 1♡, East knows that a small slam is certain and there may even be a grand slam.

If West holds all three missing kings, East wants to bid 7♡. But to find out, he must first ask West for aces, even though he holds all 4 in his own hand.

West shows 0 or 4 aces and East bids 5NT. This bid not only asks for kings, it tells West that the partnership is not missing any aces.

West shows 3 kings and East bids the grand slam.

After your partner relays how many kings he has, you must place the final contract.

There is no way to ask for queens. A bid of 6NT is always to play.

After bidding Blackwood, you may learn that the partnership cannot afford to contract for slam because you are missing an ace (or aces).

You can end the auction on the 5 level by bidding a suit which has been previously bid by one member of the partnership.

If you cannot bid the suit you want as trump because your partner's response to Blackwood has taken you past that suit, you must be prepared to play in notrump.

For example, assume you want to play in a contract with clubs as trump. If you bid Blackwood (4NT) and partner responds by bidding 5◇ (showing 1 ace) you can no longer play in 5♣ if 1 ace is not enough to bid the slam.

So you must be prepared to play in 5NT.

But you cannot bid a direct 5NT because partner will think you are asking for kings and respond accordingly.

In order to stop at 5NT, bid a new suit which has not been previously mentioned. This will alert partner that you want to play in notrump and he will end the auction by bidding 5NT.

Here is how this works:

Notes:

West (19)   East (12)

♠ K Q J   ♠ 10 5
♡ K J   ♡ A Q 3
♢ K Q J 8 6 5   ♢ A 9 7 4 2
♣ K 10   ♣ Q 6 3

1.   1D   1.   3D
2.   4NT   2.   5H
3.   5S!   3.   5NT!
4.   P   4.   ____

West needs East to hold at least 3 aces to contract for a diamond slam. When East announces only 2 aces, the final contract must be on the 5 level or the opponents will defeat it by cashing their aces.

Unfortunately, West can no longer play in 5♢ because the auction is currently at 5♡. He is willing to play in 5NT, however, and bids 5♠ (spades have not been bid previously) to give partner the message.

East is obligated to bid 5NT and West is happy to pass, ending the auction.

When East bids 5NT, it cannot be construed as asking for kings because only the person who asks for aces can ask for kings.

Also, the only time that 5NT will ask partner for number of kings is directly after partner has responded to 4NT (Blackwood).

Explanation:

The easiest slams to bid are after partner has opened in notrump.

You will know from your partner's opening his exact point range. By adding your points to his, you

A quick review:

Either the opener or responder may ask his partner for aces by bidding 4NT. This bid is called Blackwood.

The responses are:

5♣ means 0 or all 4 aces.
5♢ means 1 ace.
5♡ means 2 aces.
5♠ means 3 aces.

After partner responds to Blackwood, a direct bid of 5NT asks for number of kings.

The responses are:

6♣ means 0 or all 4 kings.
6♢ means 1 king.
6♡ means 2 kings.
6♠ means 3 kings.

You cannot ask for kings unless you have already asked for aces, and when you do ask for kings, you guarantee that the partnership is not missing any aces.

A bid of 6NT is always to play. There is no way to ask for queens.

If after bidding 4NT you want to play in a suit contract on the five level, simply bid that suit. If you want to play in 5NT, bid a previously unmentioned suit and partner will convert to 5NT.

should know whether there is a
chance for slam.

When partner opens 1NT, bid 6NT
with 16 to 18 points and 7NT with
21 points or more.

West (17)   East (17)

♠ K J 7   ♠ A Q 9
♡ A Q J 3   ♡ 8 7 6
♢ K 7 5 3   ♢ A Q J 10
♣ K 4   ♣ A 3 2

1.   1NT   1.   6NT
2.   P   2.   ____

West opens 1NT showing 16 to 18
points. East knows for sure that
the partnership has at least 33
points and that is enough to bid
a small slam.

When partner opens 2NT, bid 6NT
with 11 to 14 points and 7NT with
15 points or more.

West (22)   East (16)

♠ A K 3   ♠ Q J 8
♡ A K J   ♡ Q 2
♢ Q 10 9 6   ♢ A K 5 3
♣ K Q 3   ♣ A 10 8 7

1.   2NT   1.   7NT
2.   P   2.   ____

West opens 2NT showing 22 to 24
points. East knows that the
partnership must have all the
aces and kings and enough points
(at least 38) to bid a grand
slam.

When partner opens 3NT, bid 6NT
with 8 to 11 points and 7NT with
12 points or more.

Notes:

West (26)   East (8)

♠ A K Q   ♠ 7 5 4
♡ K Q 8 5   ♡ A 10 2
◇ A K J 5   ◇ Q 10 9
♣ A 10   ♣ Q 8 4 3

1. __3NT__   1. __6NT__
2. __P__   2. _____

West opens 3NT showing 25 to 27
points. East knows that the
partnership has at least 33
points and that is enough to bid
a small slam.

When partner opens in notrump
and you are unsure whether the
partnership has enough points
to contract for slam, invite by
bidding 4NT.

This is an instance when 4NT
would not be Blackwood--when it
is bid directly over a notrump
opening by partner.

This is called a quantitative
raise.

When partner opens 1NT, bid 4NT
with 15 points. When partner
opens 2NT bid 4NT with 10 points,
and when partner opens 3NT, bid
4NT with 7 points.

West (18)   East (15)

♠ K J 8   ♠ Q 10
♡ A 6 5 4   ♡ K Q J
◇ A J 7   ◇ K 6 4 3
♣ K Q 2   ♣ A 10 5 3

1. __1NT__   1. __4NT__
2. __6NT__   2. __P__

West opens 1NT showing 16 to 18
points but East is unsure if there
is a slam. He invites to slam by
bidding 4NT and West, with a
maximum point count, accepts by
bidding 6NT. If West held less
than 18 points, he would pass
4NT.

A quick review:

After partner opens in
notrump, add your points
to his to determine whether
or not to bid a slam.

If you are unsure whether
to bid slam, invite partner
by bidding 4NT.

This is not Blackwood. It
is a quantitative raise.
You can only invite in
notrump (4NT) directly after
partner has opened in
notrump.

Partner opens 1NT:

Bid 6NT with 16 to 18 points,
7NT with 21 points or more
and invite with 4NT holding
15 points.

Partner opens 2NT:

Bid 6NT with 11 to 14 points,
7NT with 15 points or more
and invite with 4NT holding
10 points.

Partner opens 3NT:

Bid 6NT with 8 to 11 points,
7NT with 12 points or more
and invite with 4NT holding
7 points.

Questions:

1. When can you count distributional points such as a singleton or a doubleton?

2. How many points do you count for a void?

3. For a singleton?

4. For a doubleton?

5. What are the requirements for a jump shift by the opener?

6. What are the requirements for a jump shift by the responder?

7. What do you bid when you want to ask partner for aces?

8. What is this bid called?

9. What do you bid when you want to ask partner for kings?

10. Can you ever ask for kings without first asking for aces?

11. If partner bids Blackwood and you hold 2 aces, what should you respomd?

12. When is 4NT not a Blackwood bid?

Answers:

1. Only when you have a fit with partner.

2. 3 points.

3. 2 points.

4. 1 point.

5. Opener shows 19 or more points, at least 4 cards in his second suit (usually) and a desire to explore for slam.

6. Responder shows a very strong suit or a good fit with opener, 18 or more points and a desire to explore for slam.

7. 4NT.

8. Blackwood.

9. 5NT.

10. No.

11. 5♡.

12. Whenever you bid 4NT directly over your partner's notrump opening, the bid is an invitation to bid slam and not Blackwood. This is called a quantitative raise.

Now bid these hands:

1.

Dealer: (13)

♠ K Q J 10 4
♡ A J 8
♢ Q 10 9
♣ 8 4

1.	_____	1.	_____
2.	_____	2.	_____
3.	_____	3.	_____
4.	_____	4.	_____
5.	_____	5.	_____
6.	_____	6.	_____

Responder: (9)

♠ A 6 5 3 2
♡ 9 7 6 4
♢ v-o-i-d
♣ K Q 3 2

How many extra points is this hand worth after partner opens 1♣?

2.

Dealer: (17)

♠ J 10 8 5
♡ A K 6 5
♢ A Q 10 7
♣ K

1.	_____	1.	_____
2.	_____	2.	_____
3.	_____	3.	_____
4.	_____	4.	_____
5.	_____	5.	_____
6.	_____	6.	_____

Responder: (19)

♠ A K Q 9 7 6 4
♡ Q J 4
♢ K
♣ A 2

Note: responder should jump shift at his first opportunity with a very strong suit, 18 or more points and a desire to explore for slam.

3.

Dealer: (17)

♠ K Q 10
♡ A J 8 6
♢ Q 8 6
♣ K Q 9

1.	_____	1.	_____
2.	_____	2.	_____
3.	_____	3.	_____
4.	_____	4.	_____
5.	_____	5.	_____
6.	_____	6.	_____

Responder: (16)

♠ 9 8 5
♡ K Q 10
♢ A K 10 9
♣ A 3 2

Answers:

1. <u>West</u>   <u>East</u>

    1. <u>1S</u> (46)   1. <u>3S</u> (198, 199)
    2. <u>4S</u> (77)   2. <u>P</u>

After West opens 1♠, East can re-evaluate his hand to
be worth 12 points (3 extra points for the void). He
therefore shows an intermediate response by bidding 3♠.
West bids the game and East passes.

2. <u>West</u>   <u>East</u>

    1. <u>1D</u> (47)   1. <u>2S</u> (201, 202)
    2. <u>4NT</u> (204)   2. <u>5H</u> (204)
    3. <u>5NT</u> (205, 206)   3. <u>6H</u> (206)
    4. <u>7S</u> (205, 206)   4. <u>P</u>

After West opens 1♦, East meets all requirements for a
jump shift and bids 2♠. West has a good fit and better
than a minimum opening. He knows that a small slam is a
certainty and wants to explore for a grand slam. By
using Blackwood he discovers that the partnership holds
all 4 aces and kings. He now knows that there will be a
good play for the grand slam and bids 7♠.

If the partnership were missing either 1 ace or 1 king
(it could not possibly be missing both) West would sign
off in 6♠.

3. <u>West</u>   <u>East</u>

    1. <u>1NT</u> (130)   1. <u>6NT</u> (209)
    2. <u>P</u>   2. <u>   </u>

After West opens 1NT, East knows his exact range for
point count. East adds his points to partner's and
totals enough to bid the slam, 6NT.

Approximately half of the time, your side is defending and your objective is to break the opponents' contract.

This will not be easy because the declarer has two advantages:

First, his side usually has most of the high cards.

And second, he can see his partner's cards and coordinate play between his hand and the dummy.

Defenders, however, cannot look at each other's cards.

They must use defensive signals to announce their high cards, and then use those high cards as wisely as possible.

This book will end with a brief examination of communication in defense.

You will learn to indicate your honor strength through the "size" of the card you lead.

When to lead short suits and when to lead long suits.

And you will learn to play your high cards to best advantage.

When you finish this section, you will no longer be a beginner.

Notes:

Explanation:

The defenders begin to communicate through the opening lead and continue to exchange information throughout the play.

Each time a defender leads a previously unplayed suit, he gives information to his partner.

This section will examine the rules which govern opening leads.

The same rules apply whenever either defender leads a new (previously unplayed) suit.

You will be on opening lead about one hand in four. The first problem is deciding what suit to lead.

If the contract is notrump, it is usually correct to lead your longest suit.

You want to exhaust the opponents of their stoppers in your suit. Then your small cards will be promoted into winners.

Remember, if the contract is notrump, no one can trump anything.

When you are the only one left with cards in a certain suit, those cards will all be winners once you gain the lead.

Your objective is to set up long-range tricks.

But if you are leading against a suit contract, you want to promote and cash your winners quickly, before they can be trumped.

In general, if partner has bid a suit it is correct to lead it.

It is usually dangerous to lead

If you are on lead against notrump, it is generally correct to lead your longest suit.

If you have 2 or 3 suits of equal length, you should lead the strongest.

Your objective is to set up long-range tricks.

Assume that South opened 1NT and North bid 3NT. As West you must make the opening lead:

1. ♠ J 8 7 3 2   2. ♠ K 9 8 6
   ♡ A Q 10   ♡ 9 7 5 4
   ◇ 6 5 4   ◇ 8 6 5 3
   ♣ 4 2   ♣ 7

Without anything else to guide you, you should lead a spade with both hands.

If partner had bid a suit, for example diamonds, you should lead a diamond.

If one of the opponents had bid spades, you would be better off leading another suit.

a suit when you know the opponents have length and strength in it.

But any of these rules can be disregarded if you have a good logical reason to do so.

Deciding what suit to lead is mostly a matter of judgement and developing good judgement is the hardest part of bridge.

After you have determined the correct suit, you must lead the proper card.

Each card can give a different message regarding your distribution and honor strength.

Generally: Lead top of a sequence, top of nothing and low from an unsupported honor.

One of the best leads against either a notrump or suit contract is the top of an honor sequence.

An honor sequence is two (or more) touching cards headed by a 10 or higher.

Assume you want to lead a spade from any of these possible holdings:

1. ♠ <u>K</u> Q 6 5   2. ♠ <u>J</u> 10 9 8

3. ♠ <u>Q</u> J 9 4   4. ♠ <u>10</u> 9 8 4

In each case lead the underlined card, top of the sequence.

This lead tells partner that you have the next ranking card (below) and with one exception, you deny the honor which ranks immediately above.

<u>Special</u> <u>leads</u> <u>against</u> <u>suit</u> <u>contracts</u>:

When leading against a suit contract, it is often wise to lead a short side suit (not trump).

For example, a singleton or a doubleton.

You want to become void in that suit, enabling you to trump it later.

You are on lead against 4♡:

1. ♠ <u>8</u>   2. ♠ 9 6
    ♡ A 3 2   ♡ A 7 5
    ◇ 9 8 6 5 3   ◇ 8 7 5 4
    ♣ 8 6 4 3   ♣ 6 5 3 2

With hand 1, lead your singleton spade. You hope partner can gain the lead while you still hold a small trump and give you your spade ruff.

With hand 2, lead the ♠9. <u>Always</u> lead the <u>top</u> card of a doubleton.

This time the suit must be led twice before you can trump it, but it is still your best lead.

When your doubleton is headed by the ace, it is almost as good as leading a singleton.

You will lead the ace first followed by the lower card.

When you lead the 10, you promise the 9 and deny the jack.

When you lead the jack, you promise the 10 and deny the queen.

The queen promises the jack but denies the king.

The only exception occurs when you lead the king. The king can promise either the queen or the ace or both:

1. ♠ <u>K</u> Q 6 5   2. ♠ A <u>K</u> 8

3. ♠ A <u>K</u> Q 4   4. ♠ <u>A</u> 2

Again, you want to lead a spade against the opponents' 4♡.

With hands 1, 2 and 3, you should lead the king. Partner may be uncertain regarding your exact holding, but he will be enlightened shortly.

With hand 4, you should lead the ace. The lead of an ace usually implies a doubleton and alerts partner to ruffing possibilities.

The top of a sequence lead is always good against a suit contract, but usually implies a long suit when led against notrump.

If you decide to lead a suit which has no honor cards, lead the top card in the suit. This is called "top of nothing":

1. ♠ <u>9</u> 8 6   2. ♠ <u>6</u> 3

3. ♠ <u>8</u> 6 4 3   4. ♠ <u>7</u> 6 4

In each case, lead the underlined card.

Except for a doubleton, leading the top of nothing is usually a

<u>Special sequence leads</u>:

Your sequence may occur in the middle of your suit. This is called an interior sequence and it is still correct to lead the top card:

1. ♠ K <u>J</u> 10 8   2. ♠ Q <u>10</u> 9

3. ♠ A <u>J</u> 10 9   4. ♠ K <u>10</u> 9

In each case, if you decide to lead a spade, the underlined card is the correct card to lead.

Remember, when you lead a honor card, you only deny the honor which ranks immediately above it.

Finally, if you decide to lead a suit which has two sequences in it, lead the correct card for the highest sequence:

1. ♠ <u>K</u> Q 10 9

2. ♠ A <u>K</u> J 10 9

If you are going to lead a spade, the king is correct in both cases.

passive or "wait and see" lead. This lead should not be made if you think there is a better option.

It should be mentioned that there are other methods of leading from a worthless holding.

Some players lead the lowest card and others lead a middle card.

However, the most common treatment is to lead top of nothing.

If you decide to lead a suit which holds an unsupported honor or honors (no sequence) lead a low card.

The correct lead is your fourth best card. If you held ♠ K 9 8 5 3, the king would be your first best card, and counting downward the 5 would be your fourth best.

This will help partner determine how many cards you hold in that specific suit and may even help him count your distribution in other suits.

At first you may forget to lead your fourth best, but you will begin to do so automatically as you gain playing experience.

For now, make sure that you always lead a low card from a suit which is headed by an unsupported honor or honors:

1. ♠ K J 6 5   2. ♠ Q 8 7 3 2

3. ♠ J 6 4   4. ♠ K 3 2

If you decide to lead a spade from any of these holdings, the underlined card is the correct lead.

With hands 3 and 4, you cannot lead fourth best because you only have a 3-card suit. This is

Against suit contracts:

Either defender can decide to lead trump. Usually this is done to prevent declarer from ruffing losers in the short hand (the hand which holds the fewest trump, declarer's or dummy).

Judgment in this area can be developed through playing.

The strategy behind leading low from an honor:

Whenever you lead a low card from a suit which headed by an honor (or honors) you are hoping that partner has a high card which will promote your honor into a winner.

For example, you lead the ♠3 from this suit:

♠ Q 9 8 3

If partner has the ♠K, he will play it to force out declarer's ace. You may lose the first trick, but your ♠Q will control the suit the next time it is led.

Even if your partner cannot help you with a high card, he knows that you have some strength in that suit.

This allows him an easy exit whenever he gains the lead. He can always return your suit with some degree of safety.

the only time that leading third best is acceptable.

When you lead a low card against a notrump contract, you usually promise a long suit as well as honor strength.

Therefore, you will rarely lead a 3-card suit (third best) against notrump.

There is one exception to leading low from an honor and that exception occurs only against suit contracts.

Do not lead fourth best against suit contracts when your suit is headed by the ace.

The reason is that you may lose your ace. For example, what if declarer has a singleton king?

He will win the first trick with the king and you may never score your ace because he will be able to trump it.

In notrump, you will almost never lose your ace (no one can trump it) so it is acceptable to underlead it.

Remember, these rules apply to both opening leads and any time either defender leads a previously unplayed suit.

But they should not be followed blindly. You must learn to mix common sense with correct technique.

For example, assume you are on lead against 7NT. You would not lead fourth best from a suit headed by the ace.

If you held an ace, you would defeat the contract immediately by cashing it at trick one.

A quick review on leads and opening leads:

When on lead against notrump it is usually correct to set up long-range tricks.

You should lead your longest suit. With 2 or 3 suits of equal length, lead the strongest.

When on lead against a suit contract, try to set up tricks before they can be trumped.

Lead a singleton or doubleton if you expect to be able to trump the suit later.

Lead trump to prevent declarer from ruffing in the short hand.

In general, against both suit contracts and notrump:

When partner has bid, lead his suit.

When the opponents have bid other suits besides the trump suit, it may prove dangerous to lead one of their suits.

The correct card:

Lead the top of a sequence or interior sequence.

Lead the top of nothing.

Lead fourth best (low) with an unsupported honor.

Select your lead:

1. South opens 1NT and North raises to 3NT.

   You are West and must make the opening lead.

   Underline the card you would lead with each of the four hands.

2. South becomes the declarer in 4♠ after North opens 1♡.

   You are West and must make the opening lead.

   Underline the card you would lead with each of the four hands.

1. ♠ K 8 6 4 2
   ♡ A K
   ◇ 6 5 3
   ♣ 8 4 2

2. ♠ K J 10 9 6
   ♡ A 5 4
   ◇ 8 7 5
   ♣ 7 6

3. ♠ J 8 6 4
   ♡ Q 10 4 3
   ◇ K J 9 3
   ♣ 8

4. ♠ K Q 10 9 8
   ♡ J 9 8 7
   ◇ 9 8 7
   ♣ 6

1. ♠ K 9 3
   ♡ J 6 4
   ◇ 9
   ♣ 10 8 6 5 4 2

2. ♠ 8 6
   ♡ 7 6 4 3
   ◇ A K J 6
   ♣ 7 5 4

3. ♠ 6 4
   ♡ K J 10 8
   ◇ K 9 8 4
   ♣ 10 8 5

4. ♠ 9 8 6
   ♡ Q 7 4
   ◇ Q 10 9 8
   ♣ K Q J

Answers:

1. Your objective is to try and set up long-range tricks. Therefore, you should lead your longest suit for each hand.

1. ♠ K 8 6 <u>4</u> 2
    ♡ A K
    ◇ 6 5 3
    ♣ 8 4 2

Lead the ♠4. This is a normal fourth best lead.

2. ♠ K <u>J</u> 10 9 6
    ♡ A 5 4
    ◇ 8 7 5
    ♣ 7 6

Lead the ♠J. You are leading the top of an interior sequence.

3. ♠ J 8 6 4
    ♡ Q 10 4 3
    ◇ K J 9 <u>3</u>
    ♣ 8

Lead the ◇3. You have 3 suits of equal length. Lead fourth best from the strongest.

4. ♠ <u>K</u> Q 10 9 8
    ♡ J 9 8 7
    ◇ 9 8 7
    ♣ 6

Lead the ♠K. When you have 2 sequences in the same suit, lead the correct card for the highest sequence.

2. Your objective is to set up quick winners before they can be trumped.

1. ♠ K 9 3
    ♡ J 6 4
    ◇ <u>9</u>
    ♣ 10 8 6 5 4 2

Lead your singleton diamond. You hope to ruff a later lead of the same suit.

2. ♠ 8 6
    ♡ 7 6 4 3
    ◇ A <u>K</u> J 6
    ♣ 7 5 4

Lead the ◇K. This is the exception to top of a sequence. When your suit is headed by both the ace and king, lead the king.

3. ♠ 6 4
    ♡ K J 10 8
    ◇ K 9 8 <u>4</u>
    ♣ 10 8 5

Lead the ◇4, low from an honor. Hearts were bid by the opponents.

4. ♠ 9 8 6
    ♡ Q 7 4
    ◇ Q 10 9 8
    ♣ <u>K</u> Q J

Lead the ♣K. You have 2 sequences, but the ♣K will set up quicker winners.

Explanation:

Usually your side is defending because the opponents have more high cards.

You will have few assets to help you break their contract.

For that reason, you should learn to use your high cards wisely.

There are two common situations in which it is correct for a defender to play a high card:

First, to win or attempt to win a trick.

And second, to promote or attempt to promote a winner for the partnership.

This can be very difficult because you are unable to see your partner's hand.

You will often attempt to promote a winner in his hand without knowing whether he holds a promotable card.

All you can do is play correctly and hope for the best. Learn when you should play high cards and when you should not.

In general, if you are the last person to play on any given trick, you should try to win that trick as cheaply as possible.

This is self-explanatory and requires no further illustration.

In general, if you are the third person to play on any given trick, play high. Attempt to win the trick or promote a winner for the partnership.

Notes:

West leads the ♠2 against 3NT:

                dummy
                ♠ 5 4 3

West   East
♠ K J 9 2   ♠ Q 8 7

                South
                ♠ A 10 6

You are looking at the spade suit in isolation. If you were East, you would not see either your partner's cards or the declarer's.

But the explanations in this section will display all four hands. This will help you understand the rules and why they function.

West leads the ♠2 and South plays dummy's ♠3. East must play the ♠Q. He plays high in an attempt to win an immediate trick or promote a future trick.

In this case, the queen will be captured by the ace. But East has promoted three winners in his partner's hand.

If East plays low, South wins a cheap trick with the ♠10 and retains the ♠A to win another trick.

As third hand, play high, but never play a higher card than necessary.

West leads the ♠2 against 3NT:

                dummy
                ♠ Q 9 5

West   East
♠ A 10 3 2   ♠ K J 4

                South
                ♠ 8 7 6

When you are the third person to play on any given trick, do not play high if you have no chance to win the trick or promote a winner for the partnership:

West leads the ♠J against 3NT:

                dummy
                ♠ A Q 4

West   East
♠ J 10 9 8   ♠ K 7 3 2

                South
                ♠ 6 5

West leads the ♠J and South plays dummy's ace.

If East plays third hand high, he is throwing away his honor card. His king cannot win this trick or promote a future trick when it is wasted under the ace.

Therefore, East plays low.

West leads the ♠2 and South plays dummy's ♠9. East must play the ♠J.

The jack is as high as East needs to play. If South had played dummy's queen, East would play the king.

This position is similar to finesse situations. East has dummy's queen trapped.

By playing correctly, the defenders will win 4 spade tricks. But if East wastes his ♠K, the declarer will win a trick with dummy's queen.

As third hand, finesse for a high card in the same manner as declarer.

West leads the ♠2 against 3NT:

            dummy
            ♠ K 10 8

West   East
♠ Q 9 4 2   ♠ A J 5 3

            South
            ♠ 7 6

West leads the ♠2 and South plays dummy's 6. East must play the ♠J.

This is a finesse. West led a low card which should promise an honor, and East knows that the only missing honor is the queen. Therefore he finesses by playing the jack which will win the trick.

You won't always know if your partner holds the missing honor, or if more than one is missing, which honor he holds.

But in general, it pays to finesse when you have a reasonable chance to win an extra trick.

With few exceptions, if you are the second person to play on any given trick, play low, letting partner attempt to win the trick.

South is the declarer in 3NT and leads the ♠2.

                    dummy
                    ♠ K 5 4

West   East
♠ A 8 7 6   ♠ J 10 3

                    South
                    ♠ Q 9 2

After South leads the ♠2, West must follow low.

If instead West plays the ace, he will get no value for it. South will not play dummy's king under West's ace, so West will capture only small cards.

And South will make both the queen and king for a total of 2 tricks.

If West saves the ace to capture declarer's queen, South scores only 1 spade trick.

If you are the second person to play on any given trick, play high whenever you can get full

When you are the second person to play on any given trick, play high (for no value) when it is essential to obtain the lead.

South is the declarer in 4♠ and leads the ♠2.

                    dummy
                    ♠ K 5 4

West   East
♠ A 8 6   ♠ 9 3

                    South
                    ♠ Q J 10 7 2

South leads the ♠2 and even though this is the trump suit, you are familiar with the above position.

As West you would not play your ace because you want full value for your high cards.

But what if your partner had led a known singleton earlier in the play?

Now it is necessary to rise with your ace (even for no value) to give East his ruff while he still has a trump left.

value for your high card.

South is the declarer in 5◊ and leads the ♤Q.

dummy

♤ A J 9

West

♤ K 7 6 2

East

♤ 10 8 5

South

♤ Q 4 3

After South leads the ♤Q, West must cover with the king.

West plays high because he is getting full value for his honor card.

If he plays low, South will run the queen and later finesse the jack for 3 tricks.

By covering the queen with the king, West promotes East's 10 into a third round winner.

In general, if you can cover any honor card, it is considered sufficient value to play high in second position.

This technique is often called "covering an honor with an honor."

A quick review:

In general, if you are the last person to play on any given trick, try to win that trick as cheaply as possible.

In general, if you are the third person to play on any given trick, attempt to win the trick or promote a future trick by playing high.

But never play higher than necessary.

As third hand, finesse for a high card in the same manner as declarer.

Do not play third hand high when you have no chance to win the trick or promote a future trick.

In general, if you are the second person to play on any given trick, play low.

But play high whenever you can get full value for your high card.

Or play high for no value if it is essential.

Appendix

<u>Stayman</u>: An intro-
duction to inter-
mediate bridge. A
method of reaching
a suit contract
after partner has
opened in notrump.

How to score your
bridge game

Stayman: An introduction to
intermediate bridge:

When partner opens in notrump,
he not only defines his point
count and stoppers, he promises
equal or balanced distribution.

This means he must have some
support for any suit you may
want to bid.

If your hand is also balanced,
you will be content to play in
notrump.

But if you have a long or very
long suit, you will want to play
with that suit as trump.

To do this, you must find some
way of giving partner the
message.

When partner opens 1NT, a
response of 2♦, 2♡ or 2♠ shows a
weak hand (0 to 7 points) and a
5-card or longer suit.

The opening notrump bidder must
pass, allowing you to play on
the two level with your long
suit as trump.

West (18)	East (3)
♠ K J 7	♠ 10 8 6 4 3 2
♡ A J 8	♡ Q 4 2
♦ 9 8 5 3	♦ J
♠ A K Q	♠ 9 6 4

	West		East
1.	1NT	1.	2S
2.	P	2.	

Even though West has a maximum
18 points for his 1NT opening and
an excellent fit in spades, he
passes his partner's 2♠ response
because he knows there is no
chance for game.

Remember, East promised a
maximum of 7 points and may have
nothing at all. If West takes

another bid, for example supports
his partner's spades, he may
jeopardize any chance of making
a low level contract.

By bidding 2♠, East has placed
the partnership into the best
contract.

Many beginners would be
reluctant to bid with East's hand,
but in fact, the worse your hand
is, the more you should strive
to play in a suit contract after
partner opens 1NT.

Notice that you cannot play in
2♣. A bid of 2♣ over a 1NT
opening means something else
and will be discussed shortly.

When partner opens 2NT, bid 4♡
or 4♠ with at least 4 points and
a 6-card suit. With fewer than
4 points you will have to pass
2NT.

When partner opens 3NT, bid 4♡
or 4♠ with a 6-card suit even if
you have no points.

The notrump opener will pass,
because four of either major
is game.

When partner opens 1NT, a
response of 3♣, 3♢, 3♡ or 3♠
shows at least 10 points and a
minimum of 5 cards in your suit.

This bid may show a desire to
explore for slam, but mainly it
asks the opener to choose the
best game.

If partner has a fit with your
major suit (at least 3 cards) he
will raise you to game. Otherwise
he will bid 3NT.

If partner has a fit with your
minor suit, he will raise you to

Notes:

game only with a good fit and a maximum notrump opening. (11 tricks are hard to make.) Otherwise, he will bid 3NT.

West (17)   East (11)
♠ K 4 3   ♠ A J 7 5 2
♡ A J 7 6   ♡ 10 9
◊ K Q 10 7   ◊ A 4 3 2
♣ A 2   ♣ Q 10

After West opens 1NT, East jumps to 3♠. This bid announces a hand that wants to play in game and requests West to bid the best game.

Because West has a good fit in spades he bids 4♠. If he had only 2-card spade support, he would have bid 3NT.

If East held a better hand and was thinking of slam, he would take another bid over 4♠ (or 3NT as the case may be).

If East held 6 spades, he would bid 4♠ over 1NT because he knows that partner must hold at least 2-card support for his 1NT opening.

When partner opens 1NT, a response of 2♣ is a request for opener to bid a four card major (if he has one) and does not necessarily express any interest in the club suit.

This is an artificial bid called Stayman, which will allow the partnership to play in a major suit contract whenever they have a four-four major suit fit.

You must meet two requirements before you can bid Stayman. First, you promise at least 8 high card points and, second, you guarantee at least one 4-card major suit.

Notes:

When you bid 2♣ (Stayman) you are really saying, "Partner, I think we have a chance for game in a major suit. I have at least one 4-card major and need to know if we have a fit. Do you also have a 4-card major?"

The notrump opener is now obligated to furnish the required information.

If he has a 4-card major he bids it on the two level. If not, he bids 2◊. This says nothing about his diamond holding, he is simply saying, "No, I do not hold a 4-card major."

If the notrump opener holds 4 cards in both major suits, he should bid spades first. He can always show hearts later if the opportunity arises.

If your partner, West, opened 1NT, you would bid Stayman (2♣) with each of the following hands:

1. <u>East</u> (8)
   ♠ A K 6 5
   ♡ 9 8 5
   ◊ 8 7
   ♣ J 6 5 2

2. <u>East</u> (8)
   ♠ Q 10 8 5
   ♡ J 10 9 6
   ◊ A 2
   ♣ J 3 2

3. <u>East</u> (11)
   ♠ K 10 5 4
   ♡ A 8 7 5
   ◊ A 5 4
   ♣ 3 2

4. <u>East</u> (11)
   ♠ 8 6
   ♡ Q J 10 5
   ◊ A K 8
   ♣ J 5 3 2

Each of these hands has some ruffing value and you would rather play in a major suit contract than in notrump.

On hands 1 and 2, if partner answers Stayman by bidding 2♣, you would invite to game by raising to 3♣. If the notrump

Notes:

opener holds a maximum point count (18 points) he will bid the game. Otherwise he will pass your 3♠ bid.

On hands 3 and 4, if opener bids your major, you will raise to game because even if partner holds a minimum (16 points) the combined total is still over 26 points and that is all that is required to bid a major suit game.

If the opening notrump bidder did not have a 4-card major, he would respond 2◊. You would then try for a game in notrump.

On hands 1 and 2, you would invite to game by bidding 2NT, and on hands 3 and 4 you would bid the game yourself (3NT) because you know the partnership holds enough points to make game a good proposition.

Here's how Stayman works:

West (17)	East (11)
♠ A K J 4	♠ 8 3 2
♡ K 9 8 6	♡ A J 10 4
◊ A 2	◊ K 7 6 5
♣ Q 10 8	♣ K 6

1.	1NT	1.	2C
2.	2S	2.	3NT
3.	4H	3.	P

West opens 1NT and East would like to play in hearts if his partner has a fit. He bids Stayman in order to find out.

West, holding two 4-card majors bids the spades first. Knowing that the partnership has enough points for game, but lacking a spade fit, East bids 3NT.

Now West converts to 4♡. He knows that his partner must hold at least one 4-card major to bid

Important:

Do not use Stayman with completely balanced distribution. If your 4-card major is accompanied by exactly 3 cards in each of the other suits, simply raise partner in notrump according to your point count.

Stayman and if it is not spades, it must be hearts.

When partner opens 1NT, bid 2♣ followed by 3♣ whenever you want to play on a low level with clubs as trump.

You show 0 to 7 points and a long club suit.

West (17)

♠ K Q 10 8
♡ J 7 5
◊ A K J 7
♣ K 10

East (2)

♠ 6 4
♡ 8 2
◊ 6 4 3
♣ Q 9 8 6 4 3

	West		East
1.	1NT	1.	2C
2.	2S	2.	3C
3.	P	3.	___

East knows that a notrump contract may prove to be disastrous and feels that a club contract on a low level will be much more comfortable.

He bids 2♣ and of course West thinks this is Stayman. He responds by bidding his 4-card major (spades). But when East bids 3♣ he "cancels" the Stayman.

West now knows that East has a bad hand with a lot of clubs and passes.

Important:

If partner opens in notrump and you have a balanced hand, continue to make the appropriate raises in notrump.

A quick review:

When partner opens 1NT:

Bid 2◊, 2♡ or 2♠ with 0 to 7 points and a long suit.

Bid 2♣ followed by 3♣ with 0 to 7 points and a long suit.

Bid 2♣ (Stayman) to explore for a major suit fit. You promise at least one 4-card major and a minimum of 8 points.

Bid 3♣, 3◊, 3♡ or 3♠ with at least 10 points and a long suit. This bid is forcing to game or slam.

Bid 4♡ or 4♠ with at least 10 points and a 6-card suit.

When partner opens 2NT:

Bid 3♣ (Stayman) to explore for a major suit fit. You promise at least one 4-card major and a minimum of 4 points.

Bid 4♡ or 4♠ with at least 4 points and a 6-card suit.

When partner opens 3NT:

Bid 4♡ or 4♠ with a 6-card suit, even with no points.

How to score your bridge game:

If you can find writing space on a piece of paper, you can score a bridge contest. Simply intersect two straight lines (see enclosed column) and you have your score-board.

There are four sections you can record points in, two on the left hand side and two on the right.

The left hand column is always labeled "We," the right hand column "they."

The person doing the scoring enters the partnership tallies under We and the opposition points under They.

Usually at least one partner from each side keeps score and each enters partnership points under We.

In other words, if you are keeping score, your We column should correspond exactly to the They column kept by the other side and vice versa.

Each column is divided in half by the horizontal line. Points can be entered in either the top or bottom half.

Only scores for contracts bid and made go below the line while all other points are recorded above the line.

Your object is to score two games below the line before the opponents.

We	They

This is the basic score pad used to score all games of rubber bridge. You can draw this form wherever writing space is available.

We	They
above the line	above the line
below the line	below the line

Only scores bid and made are entered below the line. All other points are written above the line.

As soon as one side has bid and made two games, the match is over.

A completed match is called a rubber and people usually play several rubbers during an evening of bridge.

The declaring side will receive a certain number of points for each trick bid and made over book.

Game is always 100 points or more recorded below the line.

Only those tricks which are bid and made in excess of book can score points below the line.

The major suits count 30 points a trick, the minors score 20 points a trick and notrump tallies 40 points for the first trick and 30 points for each trick won thereafter.

If you bid and make 4♠, you receive 30 points for each of the 4 tricks over book or a total of 120. This figure is entered in the We column and below the line.

You've just scored your first game because you've entered 100 points or more below the line.

If you don't bid to a game or slam, your contract is called a part game, part score or a partial.

It's possible to score a game by bidding and making two or more partials which together total 100 or more points below the line.

Notes:

For example, you bid and make 2♣. After giving We 60 points below the line, the opponents bid and make 3◊. This time They score the 60 points.

The first team which adds 40 points below the line will make a game.

Assume you make game first. The 60 points belonging to the opposition can no longer be used to complete a game.

Whenever either team scores a game or slam, a horizontal line is drawn through both columns underneath the score which represents the game or slam.

This line not only signifies a complete game, it nullifies any partials which have not been converted into games.

Therefore, when one team scores a game or slam, both pairs must start completely over in their quest to accumulate 100 or more points below the line.

When one team has won two games, a double line is drawn through both columns. This marks the end of the rubber.

If you win a rubber two games to zero, you receive a 700 point bonus. If the opponents have won a game, the bonus is only 500 points. These points are entered above the line.

As soon as either team wins a game they are said to be vulnerable. Both teams can be vulnerable in the same rubber. When you are in this state, game and slam bonuses are higher, but so are the penalties for failing to make your contract.

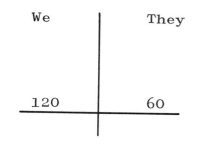

1. On the first hand, They bid and made 2♣. They score 60 points below.

2. On the second hand, We bid and made 4♡. We score 120 points below.

The line drawn under our 120 points signifies that a game has been bid and made. Both teams must now begin anew in trying to score 100 points or more, below the line.

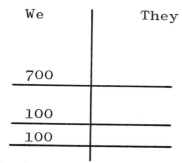

(double line ends the rubber)

1. We bid and made 3NT, scoring 100 points below.

2. We bid and made 5♣, scoring 100 points below and a 700 point bonus above, for finishing the rubber 2 games to none.

Whenever you go down in your contract the opponents will receive penalty points above the line.

Each trick you fail by is called an undertrick. The other team receives 50 points for each non-vulnerable undertrick and 100 points for every one vulnerable.

If you win more tricks than needed to make your contract, you receive trick value above the line. These extra tricks are called overtricks and score the same regardless of vulnerability.

Assume you bid 2♠ and made 3. You'd enter 60 points below the line and 30 points above.

If you bid 2NT and win 10 tricks you score 70 below (40 for the trick) and 60 above.

If the opponents are convinced that you will not make your contract, they are allowed to double you.

If you make your doubled contract, you score double the normal trick value. This means that if you're doubled in 3◊ and make it, you have just scored a game. You would get 120 points below instead of the normal 60.

If the opponents double and you think they are mistaken, you can redouble. Assuming you make your contract, each trick scores four times normal value.

If your contract was 1NT doubled and redoubled you would receive 160 points below for making it. Again, you receive credit for making a game.

	We	They
	700	
	150	
	30	200
	120	
	100	

1. We bid 4♠ and made 5, scoring 120 below and 30 below.

2. We bid 3NT and went down 2 tricks. They score 200 above.

3. They bid 3◊ and failed by 3 tricks. We score 150 above.

4. We bid and made 5◊, scoring 100 below and 700 above for completing the rubber 2 games to none.

If you are lucky enough to win overtricks in a doubled or redoubled contract, they too are worth more than normal.

Each doubled overtrick scores 100 not vulnerable and 200 vulnerable. Simply double these figures for redoubled contracts.

Whenever you play a successful doubled or redoubled contract, you receive a 50 point bonus regardless of vulnerability.

This is not doubled if the contract was redoubled. Remember, all bonuses and overtricks are entered above the line.

Of course, if you go down in your doubled or redoubled contract, the penalties are also greater.

Doubled and not vulnerable, the score 100 points for the first undertrick and 200 points for each additional undertrick.

Doubled and vulnerable, they win 200 for the first undertrick and 300 for each additional under-trick.

These rewards are doubled if the contract was redoubled.

Whenever a slam contract has been bid and made, special bonuses are given to the declaring side.

Besides the normal trick value below the line, a small slam not vulnerable scores 500 points above the line, and vulnerable, a small slam pays 750 above.

Notes:

If you bid and make a grand slam, the bonus is 1,000 points not vulnerable and 1,500 points vulnerable.

These points are given independent of the bonus received for completing the rubber, and the totals remain constant whether or not the contract was doubled or redoubled.

Whenever a rubber is left uncompleted, each team receives 300 points for a game and 50 points for a partial which could become a game if the rubber were completed.

The side which totals the most points at the end of a rubber wins it. All points are counted both above and below the line.

It's possible to make two games to the opponent's zero and still lose the rubber.

Finally, whenever any one player holds 4 out of 5 honors in the trump suit, his side receives 100 points; all 5 of the honors score 150 points. These points are always written above the line.

If the contract is notrump, all four aces (held by one player) count 150 points.

Honor bonuses are paid at any vulnerability regardless of whether or not the contract was successful. Doubled and redoubled contracts do not change the amount of the bonus.

We	They
500	
50	500
50	20
180	
	120
160	

1. We bid 3♣, were doubled, and made it, scoring 180 below and a bonus of 50 above.

2. They bid 6♦ and made 7♦. They score 120 below and 20 for the overtrick, above.

   They also score a non-vulnerable small slam bonus of 500 above.

3. We bid 2♦, were doubled and we redoubled and made it. We score 160 below and a bonus of 50 above.

   We also score a 500 bonus above for finishing the rubber 2 games to 1.

Either the declaring or the
defending side may claim honor
points. But only one player
can hold the required number of
honors.

If hearts are trump and you and
your partner each hold two of
the heart honors, your side
receives no extra points.

Do not claim honors until the
hand is over. Otherwise you give
the opponents too much
information about your hand.

When the play has been
completed, you can say, "Give me
100 honors" or "I had 150 honors."

Don't try to memorize the rules
for scoring. Instead, use the
chart which is provided on the
following page.

Eventually, you'll learn scoring
just by doing it.

Notes:

Scoring Chart:

Trick value:

Major suits – 30 points

Minor suits – 20 points

Notrump – 40 points (1st trick)
        30 points (each trick thereafter)

Only tricks bid and made over book are scored below the line. Every thing else is scored above.

Game bonus:

Finishing the rubber 2 games to 0 – 700 points
                     2 games to 1 – 500 points

Slam bonus:

Small slam non vulnerable – 500 points
            vulnerable – 750 points

Grand slam non vulnerable – 1,000 points
            vulnerable – 1,500 points

Honor bonus:

4 out of 5 trump honors – 100 points
5 out of 5 trump honors – 150 points
4 aces in notrump – 150 points

Penalties:

Each undoubled undertrick – 50 points non vulnerable
                           100 points vulnerable

Non vulnerable and doubled – 100 points for 1st undertrick
                            200 points for each trick thereafter

Vulnerable and doubled – 200 points for 1st undertrick
                        300 points for each trick thereafter

Glossary

Auction: A collective term used to describe the bidding which always precedes the play.

Blackwood (4NT): An artificial club bid which asks partner for aces. If the partnership has all four aces, 5NT now asks partner for kings.

Book: The declaring side always has a handicap of six tricks. This handicap is called book. You add book to the final level reached in the auction to determine how many tricks must be won in the play.

Broken suit: A long suit which normally plays for more than two losers.

Clockwise: To the left. Everything in bridge is done in this direction, including the deal of the cards.

Competitive bidding: When both partnerships have entered the auction in an effort to win the final contract.

Contract: The number of tricks which must be won in the play is called your contract.

Communication: The art of crossing from hand to hand. Sometimes called transportation.

Cue bid: When you or your partner bids a suit which was first mentioned by one or both of your opponents.

Dealer: The person who deals the cards at the beginning of each hand. At the end of the hand, the deal passes to the person who is sitting to the dealer's left.

Declarer: The person who will play the hand.

Doubleton: Only 2 cards in any given suit.

Double Finesse: An attempt to devalue 2 high cards held by the opponent by taking two finesses in the same suit. In cases where the 2 high cards are in sequence, the declarer can win at most 1 extra trick.

Dummy: The partner of the declarer. After the opening lead has been made, he exposes his hand face up on the table. The declarer will then play both hands.

Entry: A winning card which allows access to the opposite hand. Does not have to be an immediate winner.

Finesse: An attempt to render the opponent's high card worthless by playing for it to be in a favorable position. A 50% chance of winning an extra trick.

Fit: Whenever you and partner hold eight cards or more in a common suit, it's a fit.

Game: A designated level of bidding. If your final contract is on a game level, you receive a bonus if you make the required number of tricks.

Honor cards: The ace, king, queen, jack and ten of each suit are called honor cards. The ten is the only honor card which has no value in terms of high card points.

Honor sequence: Any two (or more) touching cards headed by at least a ten or higher. ie: ♠Q J 10 2 - The ♠Q, J, and 10 are an honor sequence.

Interior sequence: An honor sequence which occurs in the middle of a suit. ie: If you hold ♠K J 10 4, the ♠J and 10 are an interior sequence.

Jump shift: Whenever opener or responder bids by jumping over one level and shifting into a previously unmentioned suit. A strength-showing bid, always forcing to game or slam.

Long suit: Any suit which is at least 5 cards in length.

Major suit and notrump games: The major suit games are 4♡ and 4♠ and require at least ten tricks in the play. 3NT is the notrump game and needs nine or more tricks to be successful. The partnership should hold at least 26 points to contract for game in either notrump or a major suit.

Major suits: The two higher suits, hearts and spades. The suits of most importance.

Minor suit games: The minor suit games are 5♣ and 5♢ and require at least 11 tricks in the play. Minor suit games should not be bid unless the partnership holds a minimum of 30 points.

Minor suits: The two lower suits, clubs and diamonds.

Notrump: The highest step in any given level of bidding. In bridge play, a notrump contract is played without any trump or "wild cards." The highest card played of the suit originally led always wins the trick.

Opening bid (Opener): The first bid made in any auction, other than pass. The opener must have at least 13 points to open the bidding.

Opening leader: The person to the left of the declarer. He will lead the first card to begin the play. The opening lead is always made before the dummy is exposed.

Overcall: When one side bids (other than pass) after the other side has opened the bidding.

Overtricks: Tricks which are scored in excess of your contract.

Partial, also partscore or partgame: When a partnership scores a contract which is under game level in any suit or notrump.

Penalty double: A double which states that you think the opponents will not make their contract.

Playable suit: Usually a long suit (5 or more) always headed by at least the queen and jack.

Pre-empt: An obstructive bid made on a high level which makes it difficult for the opponents to enter the auction. Sometimes called a shut-out bid.

Quick tricks: Honor cards or a combination of honor cards which almost always win tricks, whether you are declaring or defending.

Redouble: A bid made when your right hand opponent doubles for take-out after partner has opened the bidding. It shows a minimum of 10 high card points and tends to deny a fit. When a redouble is employed over an opponent's penalty double, it generally means that you feel you will score your contract.

Response (Responder): When an opener's partner answers him, it is called a response. The responder needs a minimum of 6 points to respond to the opener.

Rubber: A scoring term used when one partnership scores two games before their opponents. One partnership must win two rubbers to end the match.

Ruff or Ruffing: to trump or trumping.

Sacrifice: Deliberately bidding to a contract you do not expect to make, to prevent the opponents from making their own contract.

Semi-solid suit: A long suit which usually plays for 1 or 2 losers at most.

Singleton: Only 1 card in any given suit.

Slams: A slam is a 12 or 13 trick contract which can be bid in any suit or notrump. A small slam (on the 6th level) requires 33 points, while a grand slam (on the 7th level) needs at least 37.

Solid suit: A long suit (at least 5 cards) which usually plays for no losers.

Stayman: An artificial club bid, always made on the next highest level after partner has opened 1 or 2 notrump. This bid allows the partnership to find a major suit fit.

Stopper: A protected honor card.

Suits: The 4 suits are spades,(♠) hearts (♡), diamonds (♢) and clubs (♣).

Take-out double: Sometimes called an informative double, it is usually made on a low level and asks partner to bid his longest suit.

Trick: After all four people have played a card in clock-wise order, that group of four cards is called a trick.

Tripleton: 3 cards in any given suit.

Trump: A designated suit, any card of which may win a trick if the person who holds it cannot follow suit to the trick in progress. A wild card.

Undertricks: The number of tricks by which you failed to score your contract.

Void: Whenever you have no cards in any given suit, you are "void" in that suit.